Negotiation: Theory and Practice

Organizational Behavior and Psychology Series

H. Joseph Reitz,
University of Florida
Series Editor

Group Effectiveness in Organizations

Linda N. Jewell,
University of South Florida

H. Joseph Reitz,
University of Florida

Mentoring at Work

Kathy E. Kram,
Boston University

Negotiation: Theory and Practice

James A. Wall, Jr.
University of Missouri

Negotiation: Theory and Practice

James A. Wall, Jr.
University of Missouri

Scott, Foresman and Company

Glenview, Illinois
London, England

In memory of J. Stacy Adams,
mentor, colleague, and friend

(Library of Congress Cataloging in Publication Data)
Wall, James A.
Negotiation, theory and practice.
(Organizational behavior and psychology series)
Bibliography: p.
Includes index.
1. Negotiation. 2. Negotiation in business.
I. Title. II. Series.
BF637.N4W35 1985 302.3 84-20279
ISBN 0-673-15865-9

Printed in the United States of America.

1 2 3 4 5 6-MPC-8887868584

Foreword

The new Scott, Foresman Organizational Behavior and Psychology Series offers a variety of psychological and behavioral topics at both the individual and interpersonal levels. Each book in the series provides, at an advanced level, theory, research, and organizational applications in an area relevant to human behavior in organizational settings.

The objective of each book is to bring together the relevant research and theory in an area and to demonstrate its applicability to understanding, predicting, and influencing behavior in organizations. The authors have been selected for their knowledge of their areas and for their experience in organizational applications of that knowledge.

The series is particularly designed to meet the needs of professional and graduate school students in disciplines concerned with the applications of behavioral science to organizational settings. Topics were selected for their relevance to students in such seemingly diverse areas as business, educational administration, journalism and communications, library science, medicine and dentistry, criminal justice, social and industrial psychology, civil engineering, hospital administration, military science, arts and public administration. In short, the series will be of interest in any field which now recognizes the particular need for its students and practitioners to understand and deal effectively with human behavior in organizations.

H. Joseph Reitz

Preface

This book is about negotiation—the process through which two or more parties seek an acceptable rate of exchange for items they own or control. The volume's principal goals are (1) the development of an understanding of what negotiation entails, (2) clarification of how negotiation should be used, and (3) the delineation of the merits of effective negotiation. This book is not a review of the negotiation literature or a synthesis of the various studies or findings therein. (For those interested in such an overview, I suggest Dean G. Pruitt's book *Negotiation Behavior* (1981), New York: Academic Press.) Rather, the subsequent pages offer a unique development designed to benefit academics as well as practitioners.

A succinct overview of the game plan follows. Initially, we will focus upon the negotiation concept, what it is, what determines the negotiator's behavior, and what are the different structures within which negotiation takes place. Having developed this underpinning, we will then turn to the basic problem facing negotiators: how they are to raise their outcomes in and from the negotiation. Dealing with this topic requires a thorough examination of three processes: maneuvers, tactics, and strategies. As we probe these concepts in some detail, the overall logic guiding our venture will be that the negotiator must initially choose or develop an overall strategy and then select the appropriate maneuvers and tactics for its underpinning. The selection and development of the proper negotiation strategy, along with its components, demand consideration of the situation in which the negotiation is embedded. We therefore will analyze the negotiation situation and provide guidance for the situational-contingent selection and development of a negotiation strategy. Finally, we will consider the use of negotiation in decision making, group leadership, organizational management, and conflict resolution.

This book should be of value to two groups: (1) students and researchers in the social sciences and (2) practitioners such as business leaders, hospital administrators, lawyers, journalists, and public administrators. For the first group, this volume offers coverage of topics—maneuvers, tactics, and contingent strategies—not previously dealt with in a detailed fashion by the negotiation literature and a well-developed theory of the determinants of the negotiator's behavior. For the second group, the following pages provide a no-nonsense description of negotiation, prescriptions and proscriptions for effective negotiation, and solid evidence about why administrators should improve their negotiation effectiveness.

James A. Wall, Jr.

Contents

Negotiation: Theory and Practice

Chapter 1

Introduction

Centuries ago, perhaps two millennia, on this stretch of West African coast, a fleet of six ships with triangular sails had appeared, coming through the Gulf of Guinea from the north. The men who sailed these ships were white, burned by the sun, thinned by hunger. They came ashore. They spoke an unknown language. By gesture, they asked for food and drink. It was brought, and as was the custom in that place, the ancient system of dumb barter was begun.

Grain and palm wine were set out by Ashantis, who then retreated a distance. The foreigners advanced to inspect the victuals. They put down gold coins, bars of copper, knives of bronze, strings of glittering red beads. All this was placed alongside the provisions. Then the white men retreated. The Ashantis advanced to inspect what had been left. It was not enough. They retreated in silence. The strange men came forward and added more gold coins, more bronze knife blades, and retreated once more.

This happened yet again. Then the Ashantis, satisfied with the bargain, picked up the trade goods and departed. The white men loaded their grain and palm wine and sailed away. They were never seen again. They were small men, wiry and strong, with protruding lips and long, bent noses (Sanders, 1978, pp. 96–97).

● What is a book on negotiation doing in a series like this? That is a good question, and the answer is better: negotiation is useful. Peruse any newspaper and you will note cases in which negotiations are or should be under way. The trash collectors or transit workers in a major city are on strike as their representatives bargain with city officials.

Iran and Iraq are simultaneously warring and negotiating. College draft choices and free agents are negotiating contracts. Ethiopia and Somalia fight instead of negotiating, at a cost of hundreds of thousands of lives. A major company maneuvers to effect the takeover of another. Criminals are plea bargaining, and thousands of civil cases are settled out of court.

As you observe the daily interactions of those around you, you also note many explicit and tacit negotiations. Workers jockey with their colleagues about work load, division of responsibilities, elbow room, salaries, and so on. Likewise, managers and military officers find they must negotiate with, rather than command, others of the same rank. On occasion they find that negotiation is also the best method for dealing with their subordinates and superiors. On the home front, husbands and wives constantly bargain, sometimes with each other and at times with their children. In various regions, people barter; in others, nations like Egypt and Israel negotiate, seemingly forever, but without resorting to war.

Yes, negotiation is valuable to individuals, groups, organizations, and nations. It facilitates conflict resolution, decision making, sales of goods and services, purchases, group coordination, and the management of organizations large and small. This chapter will examine some specific cases in which negotiation played a pivotal role. Before developing additional appreciation for the process, however, the meaning of *negotiation* should be clarified.

What is negotiation, and how does it differ from bargaining, trading, or haggling? Anselm Strauss (1978), using *Roget's International Thesaurus*, addressed the answer or question this way:

Negotiate—bargain, contract, arrange
Bargain—negotiate, contract
Contract—agreement, bargain, arrangement
Agreement—accord, reconcilement, understanding, contract, compact
Compact—contract, settlement, bargain, negotiation, arrangement, understanding
Understanding—compact, agreement, adjustment
Adjustment—reconcile, settle, arrange
Reconcile—adjust, settle
Settle—reconcile, fix, stabilize (see arrangement)

Arrangement—settle, organize, coordinate, orderliness
Coordinate—adjust, organize
Organize—arrange, coordinate, systematize
Systematize—arrange, organize, coordinate
Order—arrangement, systematization

Such a presentation does little to answer the questions, and neither do the varied definitions found in dictionaries, psychology texts, and negotiation monographs. However, after considering the various sources and parsimoniously compromising among them, we can define *negotiation* as a process through which two or more parties coordinate an exchange of goods or services and attempt to agree upon the rate of exchange for them. In this interaction, the primary objective may be an agreement or any other outcome indigenous to or resulting from the ongoing exchange.

Most scholars and interested practitioners at one time or another question the difference between negotiation and bargaining. The distinction will be made quite precisely later, but here it will suffice to say that negotiation is a more general category composed of bargaining and debate. *Bargaining* can be succinctly defined as moves by the negotiator to alter the opponent's behavior, whereas *debate* is the problem-solving portion of a negotiation. Debate entails discussions, explications, interpolations, syntheses, and proposals undertaken jointly by the negotiator and opponent in order to decide upon an agreement that is acceptable to both sides. Since *negotiation* indicates a more complete category of behavior, it will be the term used in the subsequent pages. It includes two facets that overlap debate and bargaining: explicit negotiation and tacit negotiation.

Explicit and Tacit Negotiation

Explicit negotiation, which is more salient and thereby better understood, is felt to be the principal underpinning for labor negotiations, diplomatic exchanges, conflict resolution, and market bargaining (Strauss, 1978). In an explicit negotiation, the parties do not necessarily act rationally or know their own and the others' preferences or values. However, they do communicate openly, making demands, stating preferences, asking for information, offering proposals, and making concessions. In so doing they maneuver, use tactics, and follow strategies that are observable by an onlooker.

In tacit negotiations, the communication is carried out in a nonexplicit form. That is, the messages are passed between or among negotiators indirectly in the form of hints, signs, and obscure intimations. As Schelling (1960) notes, this bargaining is typically used whenever communication is incomplete or impossible, whenever either party will not negotiate explicitly, and whenever neither will trust his or her counterpart in an explicit negotiation.

How do negotiators bargain tacitly? They may use words to spell out a message "between the lines," or they may rely entirely on signs, gestures, and signals. As an example of the first, most commonly employed technique, consider a settlement negotiation between two attorneys. The plaintiff's attorney is demanding a $17,000 payment, to which the defendant's attorney replies, "$17,000? We wouldn't pay you $10,000, let alone $17,000." What is the defendant's attorney writing between the lines? "Let's settle for $10,000." Or the defendant's attorney could say, "Hey, it seems like we're hopelessly deadlocked $7,000 apart on this one." Here the attorney is saying tacitly, "Let's settle at $13,500."

Japanese negotiators bargain tacitly by asking questions about the opponent's position. A question indicates some disagreement; many questions, serious disagreement. While they ask questions, the Japanese negotiators not only hint at disagreement; they simultaneously give hints as to their own position.

In the passage introducing this chapter, a tacit negotiation was conducted without any words. The natives, by leaving the sailors' offer in the sand, were unequivocally asking for a higher offer; when they gathered the items and left, they had accepted the offer.

Why do people negotiate tacitly? Sometimes communication is impossible, distrust is total, or norms exist that prohibit explicit negotiation. On some occasions tacit negotiation complements its explicit counterpart, and in most cases it avoids face loss for the interacting parties. Wartime bargaining, for instance, typically involves the first two conditions. There is no trust or communication, as the Egyptians found in the Six Day War with Israel. In the initial minutes of this war, the Egyptians occupied the Sinai and were threatening Israel's southern region; however, as Israel moved its troops against the Egyptians, they began to fall back across the Sinai toward Egypt. This retreat was costly to the Egyptians in face and matériel. To the Israelis it also had potential costs, because their supply lines were overly extended, and they knew that at some point the Egyptians would turn and fight. Both sides then wished to draw up a stationary battle line, but there was no communication and even less trust. Had there been no Suez Canal, the Egyptians would have withdrawn to Cairo and there the line would have been formed, because even without communication, both sides knew the Egyptians had to defend their capital. Fortunately, though, the Suez Canal was there. It was prominent, especially when compared with the sand on both of its banks, and it was easily crossable. The prominence and crossability of the canal permitted the two opposing armies to agree tacitly that it was to be the stationary boundary between them: The Egyptians were to retreat to the western side of the canal without much of a fight, and the Israelis were to advance only to the eastern bank. Then the battle would be converted to a shooting match.

In cases where norms or rules prohibit explicit bargaining, tacit bargaining fills the necessary negotiation role. People seldom negotiate explicitly for such things as love, loyalty, friendship, understanding, and empathy. Rules prohibit negotiations with judges for their rulings, with surgeons over their fees, supposedly with policemen over law violations, and with insurance salespeople over policy prices. Therefore, in exchanges with these parties, people turn to tacit bargaining. For example, note how a young man bargains for the affections of a young woman. He does not say, "I'll love you if you'll love me." Rather, he finds opportunities and reasons to be near her. Then he engages in activities with her: talking, going to ball games, or perhaps taking a walk. He bestows gifts (or outcomes) upon her—compliments, smiles, lunches, and free trips to the movies—hoping for some form of reciprocity. He then fishes for her reciprocity or rewards with comments such as "You're a neat person," "I had a great time this afternoon," and "Want to do this again sometime?" And the relationship evolves or dissolves. It is all so much simpler for the young and explicit. I watched two children talking last year. The boy said, "Let's be friends." The girl replied, "Do you have a swing?" "Yes," the boy answered, to which the girl responded, "OK, then."

Whereas tacit bargaining can serve alone in the exchange between parties, it most often accompanies and complements explicit bargaining (Pruitt, 1971). Within this role, the tacit component can set the stage for the explicit exchange of concessions by indicating to the opponent that concessions will be matched. As will be discussed later, neither the negotiator nor the opponent wishes to make the first concession, but each at times is willing to concede *with* the other. Thus, a tacit commitment to reciprocate the opponent's concession—such as a doctor's saying to a hospital administrator, "If I had more nurses scheduled for the second ward, I would be in a better position to sell a rearrangement of the surgery schedule to my staff''—allows the opponent to make the initial concession.

Likewise, tacit concessions, unlike explicit ones, avoid position loss. Once an explicit concession has been made, it is difficult to withdraw; however, a tacit concession does not suffer from this drawback. It can be withdrawn quite legitimately. As Pruitt (1971) notes, the negotiator who says early in a negotiation ''Let's put that issue off and come back to it later'' may never mention the issue again if he gets the concession he wants from the opponent. However, if the opponent does not concede, the negotiator can return to his earlier position by dredging up the issue he had put off.

In addition to providing the aforementioned functions, tacit negotiation also minimizes loss of face or image before the opponent. If the negotiator makes an explicit concession, there is the risk that the opponent will interpret this as a sign of weakness and become more rigid. In contrast, the tacit concession is sufficiently ambiguous to preclude increased rigidity. Because of the ambiguity, opponents proceed cautiously, for they fear they might have misinterpreted a negotiator's signal, and they know that increased rigidity on their part probably will result in the negotiator's withdrawal of the concession.

Tacit negotiation also enables both the negotiator and opponent to avoid face loss before their constituents, mediators, and other third parties. As they bargain repeatedly, negotiators develop a code to which observers are not privy. Thus, if the negotiator and opponent wish, they can appear tough to bystanders without alienating their counterpart, can explore avenues of mutual interest without the appearance of desertion, and can stall until positions dictated by headquarters soften. Looking tough is perhaps the most common goal of tacit negotiation, especially in the initial phase of the negotiation, when everyone expects everyone to be tough. Bargainers initiating their negotiations have been observed to use belligerent tacit ploys, as well as profanity that would make a sailor weep, only to walk away from the bargaining table that same evening with an agreement, laughing and congratulating each other. The bargainers had their private code, and perhaps the constituents understood. The observer could not.

It appears that a negotiation becomes more efficacious when it enters the tacit realm. As negotiators develop their own language, their intimacy increases; they trust each other more; and they develop elaborate norms that in turn enhance their bonds, privacy, and trust, as well as set the stage for improved future negotiations. To be sure, there are limits to the use of the tacit facet. Tacit negotiation cannot be relied upon entirely to hammer out a SALT II treaty, legal settlement, production schedule, or refrigerator sale, but it does complement its explicit counterpart and lubricate this often friction-ridden process.

NEGOTIATION STAGES

Tacit as well as explicit negotiations flow through different phases. After observing a number of negotiations, Douglas (1957, 1962) concluded that productive negotiations usually flow through three distinct stages. The first—establishing the negotiation range—entails a thorough determination of the range in which the negotiator and opponent will consider agreements. In this stage the bargainers succinctly identify the relevant issues or problems and then establish the range or ranges within which they will negotiate. For instance, in the first stage of the SALT II talks, U.S. and U.S.S.R. negotiators established that they would negotiate over heavy missiles, light missiles, and bombers; the United States' opening proposal included a limit of 150 on the heavy missiles, and the Soviets countered with a demand for 300, thus setting a range for the subsequent negotiation (''Who Conceded,'' 1979).

The observer can recognize this stage by the parties' tough verbiage and long speeches. The verbal gladiators threaten their opponents, emphasize the lack of consonance between themselves and the opponent, and ensure all concerned that a deadlock is inevitable. Conflict is emphasized, and the opponents stress their loyalty to their groups' positions.

Having framed the negotiation arena, the negotiators move into the next stage—reconnoitering the negotiation range—in which they probe seriously within the established range. Retreats are made from initially stated positions, and the counterpart's behavior is scrutinized for signs of a tacit or explicit concession. As they circle, the negotiators profess continued disagreement but float trial concessions that can be withdrawn quickly. The parties, as they avoid commitments, seek to solve any problems inhibiting future agreement and concomitantly attempt to reduce the range in which they are negotiating. As they seek to reduce the disagreement, however, they labor equally hard to emphasize its existence and consequences.

In reconnoitering the negotiation range and seeking their goals, the negotiators use more congenial behavior, shorter sentences, and fewer threats. As they probe, the negotiators ask questions about the opponents' positions and the outcomes that other positions would yield to them. In response to the opponents' questions, they provide information, argue their cases, and call for future concessions. The atmosphere in this stage is somewhat relaxed; the parties have established the bounds on their discussion and proved themselves as tough opponents and representatives. They now are deciding among several potential agreements, but without the stress of closing upon one that they will have to defend and live with in the future.

In the final stage—precipitating the crisis, or agreement—the parties attempt to close upon an agreement. As they attempt closure, their relationship becomes tense, somewhat uncertain, but, ironically, cohesive. They probe for actual resistance points and attempt to settle; simultaneously, they realistically examine their own flexible and rigid segments while consulting with their respective constituencies. And as the negotiators close upon the agreement, they develop a cohesive unit somewhat united against all others and resistant to their constituents and other third parties who might exert pressures upon them.

It is interesting to note that the observer can easily confuse the third with the first stage. For considerable periods in the third stage the verbal duels become quite heated, because here the negotiators are attempting to reduce general agreements to specific. They become impatient, because they perceive agreement to be close and the opponents' questions, maneuvers, and discussion to be thwarting or delaying their own goal attainment. Most important, the negotiators are tense here, because they realize that the agreement soon to be struck is one they will have to live with, abide by, and defend. They have second thoughts about commitments they have tendered; opponent offers appear less palatable; and constituent criticisms move closer.

From September through December 1980 I was teaching a graduate seminar in negotiations, and the question arose as to what stage the U.S.-Iranian hostage negotiations were in. It was about December 10, and I surmised that the negotiation was evolving from Stage 2 into Stage 3. The United States and Iran, I explained, had developed a tacit agreement about what the settlement would be, and as they were hammering out the details, the exchanges were simply becoming a little testy. Thus, it was easy to confuse this third stage with the first. One student, however, expressed the opinion that the negotiation was simply cycling back through the first stage—an argument that gained great validity when the Iranians on December 21 raised their $9.5 billion demand to $24 billion. History proved me right, but in discussing the negotiation at that time, it was very difficult to pin down the stage in which the negotiation was unfolding.

Although the three stages described do not characterize every negotiation—manager-subordinate, union steward–shop supervisor, buyer-seller, doctor-administrator, and so on—they do attest to the metamorphosis through which most negotiations tend to go. Usually, negotiations begin with an emphasis on disagreement or differences; flow into a region of coordination, decision making, or perhaps cooperation; and then close upon an agreement or deadlock (Kochan, 1980; Morley & Stephenson, 1977; Pruitt, 1971; Stevens, 1963). After the agreement, there is usually an elaboration and implementation; after a deadlock, a parting of the ways or resumption of the negotiation.

Behavior in Negotiations

To this point the chapter has defined the negotiation process, distinguished tacit from explicit negotiation, and discussed the stages through which a negotiation proceeds. It turns now to the behavior of the principals in the negotiation and the determinants of this behavior. It is informative and sobering to set the stage for this investigation by examining five real-life episodes in which negotiation played a major role: (1) the U.S.-Iranian hostage release, (2) an attempted merger by R. J. Reynolds Industries, (3) news reporting at the *New York Times* and the *Washington Post*, (4) manager-subordinate relations at RCA, and (5) the settlement of a civil suit.

U.S.-Iranian Hostage Release

What follows is a chronology of the events for the fourteen and one-half months between the hostages' kidnapping and their release (Church, 1981; Magnusan, 1981; Schorff, 1981; Skow, 1981; Talbott, 1980a, 1980b; Taylor, 1981):

November 4, 1979	U.S. embassy in Tehran is stormed; Iranian students demand that the shah be returned to Iran.
November 5, 1979	U.S. President Jimmy Carter attempts to negotiate with Iranian Prime Minister Mehdi Barzargan.
November 6, 1979	Barzargan resigns in frustration, saying that Ayatollah Ruhollah Khomeini's students, not the government, are in control of the hostages.
About November 8, 1979	Carter sends Ramsey Clark and William Miller to negotiate with Khomeini, but he will not meet with them.

November 14, 1979	Carter orders: (1) a halt on delivery of spare parts to Iran, (2) the deportation of Iranian students not complying with visa requirements, (3) a suspension of Iranian oil imports, (4) the aircraft carrier *Midway* sent to the Arabian Sea, and (5) a freeze on Iranian assets.
Prior to November 19, 1979	Palestinian Liberation Organization leader Yasir Arafat intercedes on the part of the U.S. hostages.
November 19, 1979	Khomeini releases eight black male hostages and five of seven women. Later, he hints that others will be tried.
During November 1979	U.S. Secretary of State Cyrus Vance and Iranians negotiate, with U.N. Secretary-General Kurt Waldheim as mediator.
November 27, 1979	Khomeini ends Vance-Waldheim negotiations.
December 1979	Carter expels most Iranian diplomats and asks the United Nations to impose economic sanctions on Iran.
January 1–14, 1980	Iran expels U.S. journalists.
Early 1980	West German Foreign Minister Hans-Dietrich Genscher has secret contact with Ali Akbar Tabatabai, brother-in-law of Khomeini's son.
February 23, 1980	Khomeini appears to put a hold on the negotiations, saying the hostages' fate is to be settled by the parliament, Majlis, to be elected in May. After secret meetings, Iranians are ready for secret negotiations.
March 29, 1980	In a note to Iranian President Abolhassan Bani-Sadr, Carter threatens harsh new sanctions.
March 31, 1980	The Iranian Assembly votes to take control of hostages.
April 1, 1980	Carter calls a dawn press conference to say he sees progress in the hostage affair. No one else does. He then wins the Kansas and Wisconsin primaries.
First week, April 1980	Bani-Sadr says he must have the unanimous vote of the Revolutionary Council to free the hostages.
Second week, April 1980	Carter closes the Iranian embassy in Washington, orders the remaining diplomats out, and introduces an embargo on Iran.
April 24, 1980	The rescue mission fails. Vance resigns four days later, and Iranians angrily break off secret talks.
Mid-July 1980	Hostage Richard Queen is released, suffering from multiple sclerosis.
July 27, 1980	The shah dies.

End of August 1980	Khomeini states he will not negotiate with Carter or his "henchmen."
September 9, 1980	West Germans convince Iranians to negotiate and inform Washington that Tabatabai wishes to open secret negotiations. Tabatabai establishes his credentials by telling the West Germans that Khomeini will spell out the demands for the hostage release. He also provides a text of the demands. Vance sends a letter to Iranian Prime Minister Mohammed Ali Rajai asking for hostages' release. State Department Deputy Secretary Warren Christopher and a small group set up their negotiation strategy.
September 12, 1980	Khomeini spells out conditions for release: (1) the United States will not interfere in Iranian internal affairs, (2) the United States will unlock Iran's frozen assets, (3) the United States will eliminate all economic sanctions and claims against Iran, and (4) the United States will return the shah's wealth to Iran.
September 13, 1980	The speaker of the Iranian Assembly says the United States also must apologize for its long support of the shah.
Following weeks	The Carter administration agrees in principle to meet the demands but ignores the apology requirement.
September 18 and 19, 1980	In Bonn, West Germany, Genscher arranges for Christopher and Tabatabai to meet. Christopher proposes a detailed negotiation to resolve all the issues before the hostage release.
September 22, 1980	Iraq invades Iran, and Iran switches its interest from the negotiations.
November 2, 1980	Majlis approves Khomeini's demands. Khomeini, a few days earlier, had ordered the students to turn hostages over to the government, thereby setting the stage for negotiations. Hostage families are told by the State Department to be ready for a breakthrough. Majlis adds that hostages are to be released in groups. Carter calls the Majlis vote a "significant development" and says the four conditions appear to offer a positive basis for resolving the crisis. U.S. Secretary of State Edmund Muskie says a "piecemeal" release is unacceptable.
November 10, 1980	Christopher flies to Algeria to present the first specific response to the four Khomeini demands.
About November 17, 1980	Carter hints that spare parts might be delivered to Iran if hostages are released. Bani-Sadr says the sooner the hostages are released, the sooner Iran can

Exhibit 1–3. Each Negotiator's and Constituent's Total Net Outcomes.

$$\mathbf{NO = [NO_{(Interactions)} \times P] + [NO_{(Agreement)} \times P]}$$

More specifically delineated, the net outcome is as follows:

$$NO = [(R_{nij} \times {}_{r}P_{nij}) - (C_{nij} \times {}_{c}P_{nij})] + [(R_{aij} \times {}_{r}P_{aij}) - (C_{aij} \times {}_{c}P_{aij})]$$

where

NO = Party's total net outcomes.
R_{nij} = Reward i resulting from interaction with Party j.
R_{aij} = Reward i resulting from an agreement.
C_{nij} = Cost i resulting from interaction with Party j.
C_{aij} = Cost i resulting from an agreement.
${}_{r}P_{nij}$ = Probability that R_{nij} will occur.
${}_{c}P_{nij}$ = Probability that C_{nij} will occur.
${}_{r}P_{aij}$ = Probability that R_{aij} will occur.
${}_{c}P_{aij}$ = Probability that C_{aij} will occur.

negotiation. (If no alternative negotiation is available, the CL_{alt} equals only the NO from abandoning the current negotiation.) Like the NO, the CL_{alt} is the summation of probable NOs, or probable rewards and costs (Exhibit 1–4); that is, the CL_{alt} is the total of (1) NOs resulting from *not* interacting with each party times the probability that each NO will occur, (2) the probable NOs resulting from *not* being a party to an agreement, (3) the probable NOs resulting from interacting with alternative parties, and (4) the probable NOs from agreeing with alternative parties.

If the negotiator's or constituent's NO equals or exceeds his or her CL_{alt} ($NO \geq CL_{alt}$), the party will continue to participate in the negotiation, probably until an agreement is reached and implemented. However, if the NO does not equal the CL_{alt} ($CL_{alt} > NO$), the party will take steps to raise the NOs and probably will withdraw from the relationship.

Effects of NO, CL, and CL_{alt}

The manner in which the NO, CL, and CL_{alt} affect the negotiator's, opponent's, and constituent's behaviors can be illuminated further by considering the relative positions of these constructs in an actual negotiation, a settlement negotiation between the plaintiff's and defendant's lawyers. Assume that the case is a simple suit in which the

Exhibit 1–4. Each Party's Comparison Level of Alternatives.

$$CL_{alt} = \left(NO_{\substack{\text{Not interactiong with}\\ \text{current parties}}} \times P\right) + \left(NO_{\substack{\text{Not being a party}\\ \text{to agreement}}} \times P\right) + \left(NO_{\substack{\text{Interacting with}\\ \text{alternative parties}}} \times P\right) + \left(NO_{\substack{\text{Agreeing with}\\ \text{alternative parties}}} \times P\right)$$

More specifically,

$$CL_{alt} = [(R_{\bar{n}ij} \times {}_rP_{\bar{n}ij}) - (C_{\bar{n}ij} \times {}_cP_{\bar{n}ij})] + [(R_{\bar{a}ij} \times {}_rP_{\bar{a}ij}) - (C_{\bar{a}ij} \times {}_cP_{\bar{a}ij})] + [(R_{nik} \times {}_rP_{nik}) - (C_{nik} \times {}_cP_{nik})] + [(R_{aik} \times {}_rP_{aik}) - (C_{aik} \times {}_cP_{aik})]$$

where

CL_{alt} = Comparison level of alternatives.
$R_{\bar{n}ij}$ = Reward i resulting from not interacting with Party j.
$R_{\bar{a}ij}$ = Reward i resulting from not being a party to an agreement.
R_{nik} = Reward i resulting from interaction with Alternative Party k.
R_{aik} = Reward i resulting from an alternative agreement with Party k.
$C_{\bar{n}ij}$ = Cost i resulting from not interacting with Party j.
$C_{\bar{a}ij}$ = Cost i resulting from not being a party to an agreement.
C_{nik} = Cost i resulting from interaction with Alternative Party k.
C_{aik} = Cost i resulting from an agreement with Alternative Party k.
${}_rP_{\bar{n}ij}$ = Probability that $R_{\bar{n}ij}$ will occur.
${}_cP_{\bar{n}ij}$ = Probability that $C_{\bar{n}ij}$ will occur.
${}_rP_{\bar{a}ij}$ = Probability that $R_{\bar{a}ij}$ will occur.
${}_cP_{\bar{a}ij}$ = Probability that $C_{\bar{a}ij}$ will occur.
${}_rP_{nik}$ = Probability that R_{nik} will occur.
${}_cP_{nik}$ = Probability that C_{nik} will occur.
${}_rP_{aik}$ = Probability that R_{aik} will occur.
${}_cP_{aik}$ = Probability that C_{aik} will occur.

plaintiff is suing the defendant. If the lawyers reach an agreement in the settlement negotiation, the defendant will pay the plaintiff the stipulated sum, and the lawyers will collect their fees. The plaintiff's lawyer can receive a certain percentage of the settlement or be paid so much per hour of invested time, whereas the defendant's lawyer will be paid by the hour. If the lawyers do not agree, the case will be scheduled for a trial; the lawyers will have to invest more time and effort, and then the outcomes will be in the hands of the judge or jury deciding the case.

Note how the NO, CL, and CL_{alt} of the plaintiff's lawyer and their relative positions (Exhibit 1–5) would determine her behavior. In Situation 1, her NO exceeds her CL—perhaps because the defendant's lawyer wants a quick settlement and thus has made a generous opening offer—and thus she is satisfied with the potential NOs and

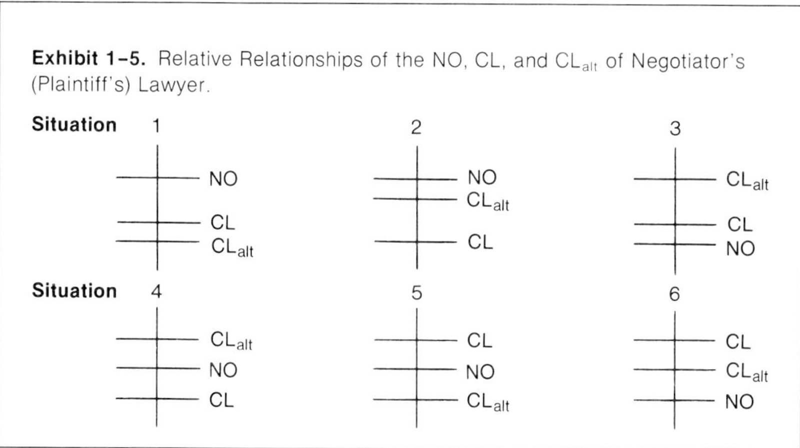

Exhibit 1-5. Relative Relationships of the NO, CL, and CL_{alt} of Negotiator's (Plaintiff's) Lawyer.

probably will not take vigorous steps to raise them. Since the NO also exceeds the CL_{alt} (that is, the expected payoff from going to trial), she probably will quickly agree. This CL_{alt} could be low because the trial would require a good deal of time and the lawyer is on a fixed-percentage agreement or because the lawyer knows that a similar case did not fare well in this same court.

Turning to Situation 2, the plaintiff's lawyer also is likely to be satisfied with a settlement, since $NO > CL$; since $NO > CL_{alt}$, she will probably quickly agree with the defendant's representative. In fact, since her aspirations are so low, she will be happy with either the negotiated settlement or the trial. However, the lawyer is likely to choose the settlement (NO), because it offers a higher probable outcome than does the trial (CL_{alt}).

Situation 3 is less splendid. Here the settlement negotiation process is proffering low outcomes to the plaintiff's lawyer. The reasons for this could be manifold: The defendant's lawyer perhaps is making low offers and smaller concessions. In addition, she might be a totally unpleasant person to deal with. The low NO could be a result of the plaintiffs themselves, who are constantly badgering their lawyer to ensure that she does not sell them out behind closed doors. The CL_{alt} could be high for the lawyer because she knows that in front of a jury she can prove herself to her clients. She feels that she can glean some favorable rulings from the presiding judge, or she expects to generate more funds for herself by devoting much time to the trial and thereby obtain a large fee (if she is paid on an hourly basis). Without a doubt, the lawyer will opt for trial here. There is a higher expected payoff from the trial; also, as can be noted, since the NO does not meet the lawyer's aspirations, she is highly dissatisfied with the current negotiation.

In Situation 4, the lawyer will be satisfied with settlement negotiation, its process, and its probable outcomes, but in spite of this satisfaction will opt for trial. The excess of CL_{alt} over the NO provides this impetus; that is, the trial offers higher probable NOs than does the current negotiation.

Situations 5 and 6 offer perhaps the most interesting sets of relationships for discussion. In Situation 5, the lawyer is dissatisfied with the negotiation because it is not panning out; that is, it is not meeting her goals or aspirations. Unfortunately, it is providing higher payoffs than she thinks a trial would; therefore, she will not abandon the negotiation and opt for trial. What will transpire here? Probably the lawyer will attempt to raise her NOs. As can be noted in Exhibit 1–3, the avenues for doing so are multiple: The lawyer can raise the fee she charges her clients. She can spend more time on the case. She can heighten her attacks on the defendant's lawyer, attempting to drive down that lawyer's CL. Or she can threaten the defendants themselves in hopes of effecting a large payoff from them.

Most likely, the plaintiff's lawyer's CL will decline in Situation 5. As the lawyer perceives that the NOs from the negotiation are not what she would like them to be and that the outcomes from the trial are even worse, she will adjust her aspirations to better fit the realities of the situation.

The aspiration level will probably fall also in Situation 6. Here the plaintiff's lawyer is dissatisfied with the negotiation because the outcomes from it do not meet her aspirations. As opposed to Situation 5, however, the lawyer here is not trapped in the negotiation; the trial holds better returns for her, so she will spring for trial. As an aside, it is worth noting that after opting for trial, the CL_{alt} becomes the plaintiff's lawyer's NO; thus, she will fight very hard to raise the CL_{alt} (that is, the total NOs of the trial) to her aspirations.

Constituents

Authors discussing negotiations almost without exception adopt the perspective taken in the previous section—that of the negotiator. Such a concentration, unfortunately, neglects the constituents' roles, despite the fact that in most negotiations and all organizational negotiations, at least one constituent observes or participates in the process. To assist in the development of a more balanced overview of the negotiation process, this section examines some of the situations in Exhibit 1–5 through the eyes of a constituent. Consider the behavior of a pathologist whose department head is negotiating with the hospital director over a budget cut to be forced upon the pathology department. If the pathologist (constituent) faces a situation like Situation 1 in Exhibit 1–5, he will be satisfied with the leader's performance. (Perhaps the NO to the pathologist represents a two-person reduction in his technical staff and a 5 percent salary increase for himself. His aspirations, CL, were for a four-person cut and a 2 percent salary increase for himself. And a position he can obtain elsewhere, CL_{alt}, entails a staff equal to a 5-person cut and no salary increase.) No doubt the pathologist will congratulate and reinforce his director. Since his own NO is greater than the CL_{alt}, he will not abandon the relationship with the department head.

In contrast, consider Situation 4. In this case, NO exceeds CL; that is, the department head is delivering more than the constituent expected. However, the alternatives exceed the probable outcomes, with the result that the pathologist will probably exit from the situation, taking advantage of the alternative. The preceding sentence intentionally includes the word *probably*, for there are other rational behaviors open to the pathologist. He can pressure the department head to negotiate more toughly so as to raise the pathologist's NO. Or he can choose as his alternative course of action the replacement of his department head with a more "effective" negotiator and thereby attempt to raise his CL_{alt}.

In Situation 5, the pathologist will be dissatisfied with the results and no doubt will pressure the department head to be more effective. Given that the alternatives are low—perhaps in terms of job opportunities and new department heads—the pathologist will not abandon the current relationships. Feeling somewhat trapped, he will have no recourse other than raising his NO. As noted before, he could attempt to influence his negotiator (department head), but his influence attempts are not limited to this sphere. He could operate directly with the hospital head (opposing negotiator), or he could make a direct appeal to the hospital board of directors (opposing negotiator's constituency).

Other Paradigms

The preceding discussion has considered the negotiator and constituent roles to be occupied by one party; however, these roles can be filled by several parties. Likewise, although Exhibit 1–1 presented a paradigm consisting of two negotiators, two constituents, and six relationships among them, this is but one situation found in negotiations. Others can be composed of more or fewer roles and more parties per role. Consider some of the following alternatives.

The simplest alternative is one made up of a negotiator and opponent, an example being the negotiation between two secretaries as to how they will divide the departmental responsibilities such as typing, filing, and telephone answering. A more expanded paradigm would emerge if one of the negotiators had a constituent. An unmarried person in a negotiation with a discount store appliance salesperson illustrates this case. The salesperson here represents and must answer to a superior, whereas the purchaser has no such responsibilities. (Here we find that the NO accruing to each party—negotiator, opponent, and constituent—is the result of the party's interaction with two others.) Giving the purchaser a spouse to whom he or she must answer forms a two-negotiator–two-constituent paradigm.

Conceptionally and realistically, more complex paradigms do exist. The constituents can have constituents themselves. For example, when Henry Kissinger negotiated with the North Vietnamese, his constituent, President Richard Nixon, closely followed his progress. In turn, Nixon himself was responsible to a constituency, the U.S. public.

More complexity is afforded by the paradigm in which the negotiator (or opponent) reports to multiple constituencies—constituencies who can have different interests and communicate different demands to their negotiator. In the hospital director–pathology head negotiations, for instance, the hospital director no doubt had multiple, diverse constituents. This director had to please the hospital board by negotiating a budget cut, yet the surgeons surely simultaneously desired that rapid and high-quality support from the pathology staff be retained. Likewise, other departments probably demanded that the hospital director not trade any of their personnel, territory, or privileges to the pathology department in order to obtain the necessary budget reductions. And the patients, and in turn the general community, served as second-order constituents demanding that the negotiation and any agreement struck be ethical and not endanger them (for example, the hospital director cannot agree that the pathology department eliminate some of its slower analyses or hire undertrained personnel to perform them).

Additional roles are formed within the paradigm when a third party such as a mediator, arbitrator, or intermediary intervenes in the negotiation, and each of these in turn may have a constituency. For instance, in the newspapers case it was noted that the managing editor at times had to intervene in the editors' space negotiations; when he mediated, he no doubt brought the influences of his constituency (the publisher) to bear.

Instead of taking on or generating new roles, the additional parties can occupy existing ones. That is, each of the roles—negotiator, constituent, mediator, mediator's constituent, and so on—can be occupied by several parties. For example, five- to twenty-person negotiator teams bargain in the United States' behalf over the terms of base locations in foreign companies. And for many unions, the entire rank and file serves as the constituency, voting upon the ratification of the contract agreed upon by its negotiators.

Summary

The previous pages have described the negotiation process, distinguished between tacit and explicit negotiation, and discussed the stages in the negotiation. Having laid this foundation, the chapter looked at some real-life negotiations and then argued that the behavior of each party in such affairs is determined by his NO, CL, and CL_{alt}. Each party (for instance, the negotiator) attempts to raise his NO as he interacts directly and indirectly with the others. If he raises his NO above his CL, he will be satisfied with his role in the negotiation. If he manages to hold the NO above the CL_{alt}, he will remain a party to the negotiation.

How does the negotiator raise the NO high enough to meet his aspirations and exceed the proceeds from other arrangements? This question brings us to a consideration of the negotiator's strategies, tactics, and maneuvers.

Chapter 2

Strategies, Tactics, and Maneuvers: An Overview

● As do the parties in any exchange relationship, negotiators attempt to raise their outcomes by giving rewards or benefits to the others—principally to the opponents. Since these conceded benefits usually prove costly to negotiators, they must consider the rewards accruing to them in light of the costs paid and then seek a favorable rate of exchange between the benefits given to the opponents (costs to negotiators) and the opponents' benefits traded to them. The overall procedure through which negotiators pursue this goal entails a weaving of tactics and maneuvers into a viable strategy.

A Visual Mapping

To portray the strategic process, we can borrow and modify a device used in economics, the Edgeworth Box (Chipman, 1965). For simplicity, consider that the negotiator is interacting with only one other party, the opponent. They wish to exchange two items, X and Y (for example, money and labor), which both possess. Exhibit 2–1 depicts the two individuals and their preference curves. For our purposes, the axes represent the amount each party *gives* to the other, and the curves represent the preferences of the two parties. Consider first the preferences of the negotiator. Probably his highest preference is Point d, at which he gives nothing to the opponent, and his lowest preference is Point g, at which he gives all the X and Y to the opponent. Analogously, the same is true for the opponent: he prefers Point h, at which he gives nothing to the negotiator. His lowest preference is Point o, at which he gives all of both X and Y to the negotiator.

Exhibit 2–1 as drawn and explained simply indicates that the negotiator and opponent are not benevolent. *Ceteris paribus,* they wish to keep their goods. Included in the exhibit are modified indifference

Exhibit 2–1. Negotiator's and Opponent's Preferences.

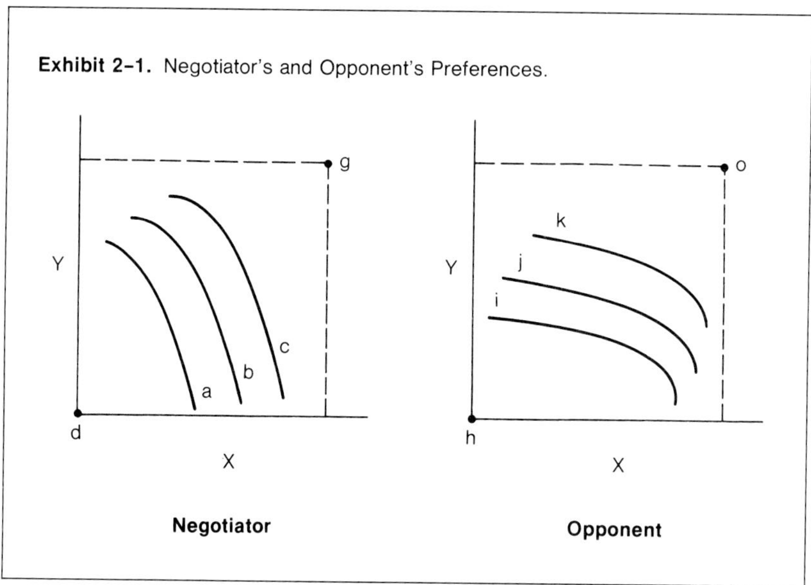

curves that indicate that the parties' preferences for the two goods differ; the negotiator has a higher preference for X and the opponent has a higher preference for Y. If we rotate the opponent's axes 180 degrees and connect them to those of the negotiator, we form a modified version of the Edgeworth Box, depicted in Exhibit 2–2. The axes now represent the combined total amounts of X and Y possessed by the negotiator and opponent.

With regard to preferences, both the negotiator and the opponent again would wish to have all of X (both their X plus that of the other) and all of Y (both their Y plus that of the other). Their preferences are still represented, with the negotiator having a higher preference for X and the opponent, for Y.

Two major features of Exhibit 2–2 are important. First, note the points at which the indifference curves touch; these connected points indicate the divisions of X and Y at which the *joint* satisfaction for the negotiator and opponent are at a maximum. Therefore, if the negotiator and opponent wish to maximize their joint outcomes, they will attempt to agree at one of these points. Second, the closer the agreement point is to each party's origin, the greater is the satisfaction.

In summary, any point of the graph is a potential agreement point. The closer the point is to Line qs, the higher is the joint satisfaction;

Exhibit 2-2. Negotiator's and Opponent's Preferences (Modified Edgeworth Box).

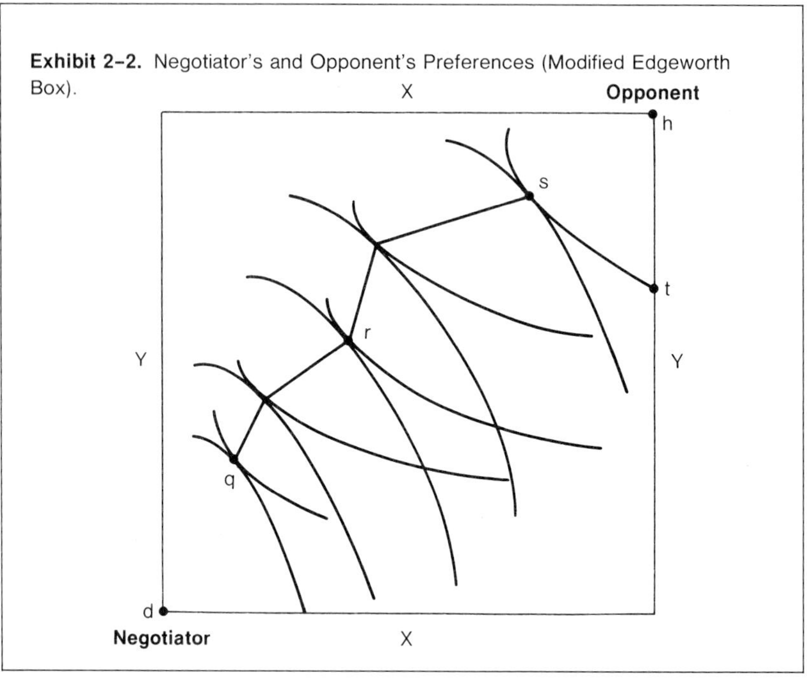

the closer it is to the party's origin, the higher is that party's satisfaction. For example, Point q maximizes the joint satisfaction for the negotiator and opponent and is clearly to the negotiator's liking. In contrast, Point d is more to the negotiator's advantage, and thus he prefers it to Point q.

Given that the negotiator prefers agreement at points that allow him high outcomes, and the opponent also prefers agreement at points yielding high outcomes to him, how does the negotiator proceed? That is, how does the negotiator get the opponent to proceed from the point that the opponent prefers to one that is acceptable to the negotiator? He uses maneuvers, tactics, and strategies.

An elaboration or modification of Exhibit 2-2 allows us to flesh out this last statement. Assume that the negotiator optimistically wishes to have an agreement at Point d, but an agreement there requires that he somehow move the opponent very far from his current location (for example, Point u). Realistically, the negotiator does not seek agreement at Point d, for his CL is not that high. Perhaps information he possesses or past experience have led him to establish his CL at the position indicated by the dashed line in Exhibit 2-3. Thus, he wishes to *move* the opponent to some point within the shaded area wherein the negotiator's outcomes (X + Y) will equal or exceed his CL. How does he do so? First, he employs techniques that foster the

Exhibit 2–3. Negotiator's Comparison Level.

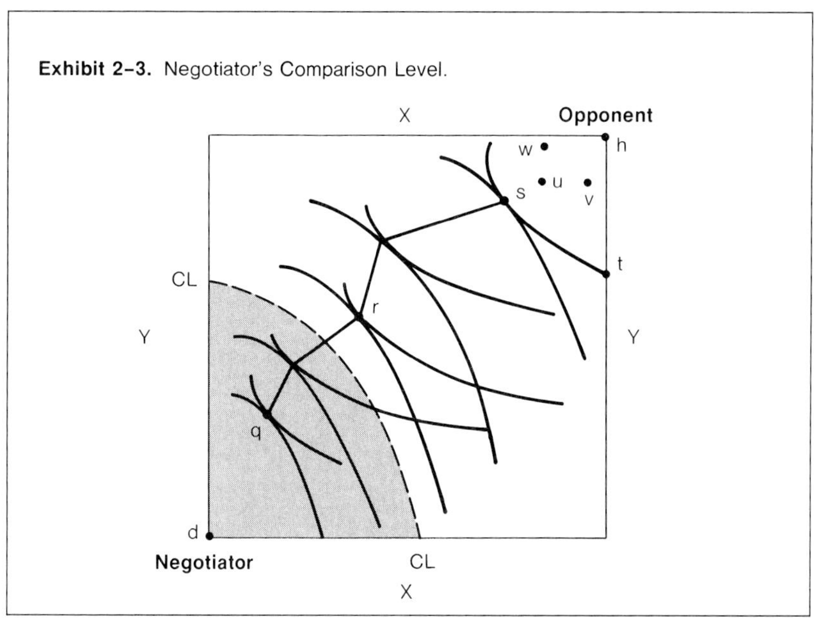

opponent's movement (that is, toward the negotiator's CL); then he can use others to guide the opponent; and, finally, he constrains the opponent's movements (for example, he prohibits regression to Point h or movement toward Points v or w) with other techniques. In short, the negotiator moves, directs, or constrains the opponent to his own benefit. How does he do so? He uses maneuvers, tactics, and strategies, seeking to apply those that are most effective and least costly to himself. The following pages will examine these processes in detail, yet before doing so it is useful to catch a brief overview of their differences.

Negotiation Strategy and Tactics

A *negotiation strategy* is the broad plan or technique used to obtain the outcomes desired from the negotiation and the resultant agreement. *Tactics* generally are considered the components of the strategy. Our understanding of a negotiation strategy and its relationship to tactics perhaps can be aided by considering examples of strategies and tactics found in other areas.

In World War II, for example, the United States' joint chiefs had to develop a war strategy. The leading alternatives were (1) a pursuit of a two-ocean offensive war or (2) a defense in the Pacific plus an offensive role in Europe. As history has recorded, their choice was the former.

Having decided to pursue the offensive role in the Pacific, a strategy was developed for conducting this campaign. In a sense, it was a double-pincer strategy, with Admiral Chester W. Nimitz and General Douglas MacArthur both swinging north toward Japan. Nimitz headed the eastern pincer, closing in through the Gilbert, Marshall, and Mariana islands. Starting in Australia, MacArthur commanded the western pincer, moving up through New Guinea, the Palau Islands, the Philippines, and Formosa. Both MacArthur and Nimitz developed a strategy for his pincer. MacArthur's was an island-hopping strategy, bypassing the strongly fortified islands and landing troops on the weaker. In this strategy, the tactics entailed storming the beaches en masse (instead of infiltrating or using an air drop), annihilating the enemy (instead of pushing it back or establishing a defensive perimeter), and developing airstrips on the islands (instead of using the islands only as supply depots and launching points).

As can be seen from this example, a *strategy* is a broad plan directed toward a specified goal, and the *tactics* are activities in pursuit of the objectives necessary to the success of the strategy. A second, and perhaps simpler, example illustrating the relationship between strategy and tactics is the organization of a socialized economy.

First comes the question of the economic goal. Is there to be a concentration upon consumer goods (for example, food, wine, and napkins), capital goods (for example, steel plants, assembly machines, and beer canners), or infrastructure (for example, bridges, roads, and electrical systems)? If the goal chosen is consumer goods (as Soviet premier Nikita Khrushchev decided in his early years), a broad strategy must be adopted to raise consumer demand, direct steel toward tractors instead of I beams, and expand distribution outlets. To fulfill the facets of this strategy, various tactics are required. To raise consumer demand, advertising might be tried. However, simply raising consumer incomes might suffice.

Negotiation Maneuvers

If the strategy is a broad action plan and the tactics are the specifics for that plan, what is a maneuver? It is *not* a subtactic.

Succinctly defined, a *maneuver* is a behavior undertaken to improve one's position for the defense or offense. Accounts of sea, air, and land battles contain classic examples of maneuvers. The captains of the Greek triremes maneuvered their oar-driven vessels so as to gain maximum speed and then ram their bows into the opponents' broadsides. Several centuries later, captains of the wooden men-of-war developed the opposite maneuver. They moved their ships so that they exposed their broadsides, and thereby one-half of their barrels, to their opponents' unarmed bows. As for the captains today, they learn quite soon to sacrifice distance for the port tack advantage in the sailing battle.

In the air, German ME-109 pilots always maneuvered their planes above B-17s and between the bombers and the sun so that they could speedily attack the "flying fortresses," whose crew thus faced the disadvantage of having to look and shoot into the sun. On land, "take to the high ground" has been the classic maneuver for the offense or defense. Generals mass their troops (or, as in the case of Chinese Red Army Field Commander Lin Piao, disperse them) in order to set the battle stage to their advantage. And armies move repeatedly in order to secure optional escape routes.

The definition of *maneuver* and the previous examples provide an intuitive sense of what negotiation maneuvers entail. To add specificity, we can add that negotiation maneuvers entail behaviors undertaken by negotiators (or other negotiation parties) to improve their positions. In turn, the improved positions resulting from these behaviors can be used as an underpinning for a tactic (that is, a tactical maneuver) or a strategy (that is, a strategic maneuver).

A Brief Road Sign

How negotiators improve their positions is the topic of the next chapter. Before moving along that avenue, it may be useful to map out the remainder of our journey. Looking back, Chapter 1 delineated the bargaining process, defining the negotiation concept, outlining the negotiation stages, enumerating the determinants of the parties' behavior, and delineating the paradigms in which negotiation can unfold. The current chapter mapped out a general understanding of the concepts *strategy, tactics,* and *maneuvers.* Chapter 3 will develop a more thorough understanding of negotiation maneuvers and examine the numerous maneuvers available to the negotiator. Chapter 4 focuses on negotiation tactics, delineating and categorizing the plethora of routes open to the practicing negotiator. Chapter 5 takes up the negotiation strategies, noting those that have been tested for effectiveness and proposing others available for use in negotiations. Since a negotiator, in choosing a strategy, must match it correctly with the situation, Chapter 6 looks thoroughly at the situational aspects to be considered and guides the negotiator in the choice and utilization of the appropriate strategy. Finally, Chapter 7 enumerates the arenas in which effective negotiation proves beneficial.

Chapter 3

Negotiation Maneuvers

● The definition and examples of maneuvers supplied in Chapter 2 provide an intuitive feel for negotiation maneuvers and pave the way for a more specific discussion of these multifaceted behaviors. A simple piece of recreational equipment, the seesaw, serves as a concrete aid. Assume you and an opponent agree to compete next week in a simple bit of physical competition. You will venture to the playground and take one end of a twelve-foot seesaw in your hands, and your opponent will grasp the other. You then will compete to determine who can raise his or her end the highest. Since the seesaw is secured in the middle by a pin (Exhibit 3–1), the friendly competition promises to be a test of your relative strength and endurance—a kind of body Indian wrestling.

In preparing for this competition, you can undertake three types of maneuvers to improve your position. First, you can increase your own strength (for example, working out with weights or by drinking beer and eating pasta the night before the big event). Second, you can attempt to weaken your opponent's actual strength, perhaps by having a friend engage your opponent in a few sets of tennis prior to the match. Third, you can alter the leverage between the two of you; that is, you could arrive early and reset the pin on the seesaw so that your opponent's end is shorter than yours. In this maneuver, your strength and that of your friendly opponent remain unaltered; however, your strength is positioned advantageously. The situation is similar to that of two 1780 men-of-war: both might have 120 guns, but one is definitely positioned advantageously if its starboard side is facing the unarmed bow of the other.

Exhibit 3–1. Negotiator Playground Maneuvers.

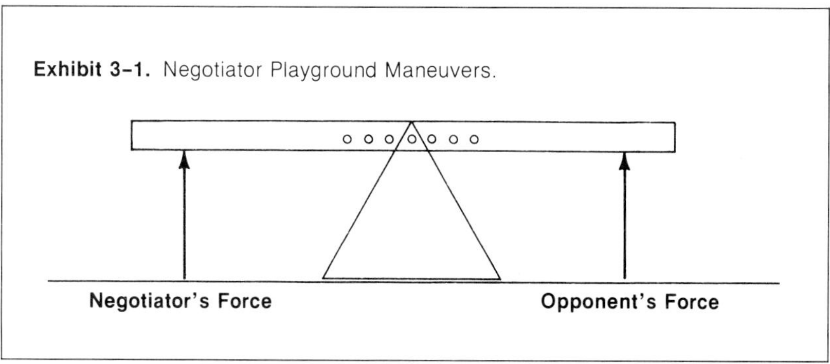

Like the playground maneuvers, those to be found in negotiations can be divided into three classifications: (1) those that increase the negotiator's strength, (2) those that reduce the opponent's strength, and (3) those that provide leverage to the negotiator (Exhibit 3–2). Most of the negotiator's maneuvers attempt to increase his or her own strength. This is not surprising, since, everything else being equal, it is better to be strong than weak in a negotiation. Strength better enables negotiators to obtain concessions from opponents; it also enables negotiators to be flexible—to make concessions themselves without the fear of subsequent exploitation by opponents.

Increasing the Negotiator's Strength

To increase their strength, negotiators can acquire status or develop abilities and skills that are of value to opponents (Tedeschi & Bonoma, 1977). Likewise, they can voice disclaimers to prevent any future loss of status (Brown, 1977) or make themselves less vulnerable by strengthening the logic of their arguments and increasing the size of their bargaining teams. In addition, negotiators can gain credibility by going on the record in the negotiation (Kissinger, 1979).

Perhaps one of the simplest, but most effective, strength-building maneuvers entails stockpiling, a move in which negotiators accumulate resources prior to and during the negotiation that will prove useful as they bargain. The stockpile can consist of the goods and services being negotiated, or they can be outcomes the opponents' services provide.

Exhibit 3–2. Negotiation Maneuvers.

Increase Negotiator's Strength	Reduce Opponent's Strength	Alter Relationships of Strength (Leverage)
Acquire status Develop abilities and skills Voice disclaimers Strengthen logic Increase size of bargaining team Go on record Stockpile Strengthen stand with constituency Make cooperative arrangements with third parties Develop outside options	Close opponent's outside options Prevent opponent's coalitions, alliances, and support Weaken opponent's stand with his or her constituency Disorganize opponent's constituency Reduce opponent's status or expertise Prevent opponent from establishing commitments Recruit opponent's associates Utilize informant	Move to address opponent's weak point Protect negotiator's weak point Wait until opponent is vulnerable Make end run Flank the opponent

(For example, the steel firms, prior to the negotiations with the steelworkers in the 1960s, stockpiled finished steel.) Adopting an opposite tack, negotiators can stockpile bargaining chips that are tradable to opponents or can be cashed in with their own constituencies.

At times shrewd negotiators will acquire chips from their constituencies, stockpile them, and then trade them to the opponents for chips the negotiators can use as leverage with their constituencies. For instance, Lyndon Johnson found that his power in negotiations with foreign states was greatly enhanced by the credits he had accumulated by granting favors to members of Congress, and, in turn, his prestige with Congress was enhanced by his successful foreign relations.

In addition to stockpiling, strengthening their stand with their constituencies is one of the most potent and essential strength maneuvers negotiators can undertake. They can meet on a one-on-one basis with the constituents, meet as a team, or even meet in a rally to convince the constituents of the value of the negotiation, to alter their perceptions of the process, or to persuade them that the tactics being pursued are correct. In the negotiation that unfolded between the Solidarity Union and the Polish government in early 1981, there was a striking similarity between the strength maneuvers of the two opposing negotiators. Lech Walesa, the negotiator for Solidarity, wanted the union to adopt a two-stage strike to demonstrate its support of his demands for the dismissal of officials responsible for the beating of local union leaders in Bydgoszcz. He threatened to resign if the union failed to support him ("Polish Unions," 1981). A few weeks earlier, his opponent, Stanislaw Kania, the head of the Polish Communist Party, had mounted the podium to call for support from the party for the measures he had taken in the negotiations with Solidarity. Like Walesa, Kania threatened to resign if he were not supported.

Another maneuver negotiators often employ is the establishment of cooperative arrangements, bonds, alliances, and coalitions with third parties. Negotiators can bribe third parties to gain their assistance, negotiate with them, threaten them, reward them, or use any of their other power bases—referent, expertise, co-oriented, or legitimate—to strengthen the ties against their opponents.

As negotiators strengthen their ties with constituencies and other third parties who can be of assistance to them, they also can maneuver to develop outside options for themselves—that is, raise their CL_{alt}. Increasing their options decreases the negotiators' dependence ($NO - CL_{alt}$) on the negotiation and thereby raises their strength relative to the opponents'. The importance of this maneuver can be seen in various negotiation settings. For instance, in a settlement negotiation, both the plaintiff's and defendant's attorneys keep open their alternative to the negotiation—going to trial—in order to strengthen their positions. Likewise, purchasing agents in negotiations with suppliers always strive to find alternative sources in order to strengthen their side in the negotiation with the current supplier.

Decreasing the Opponent's Strength

Although negotiators maneuver most frequently to increase their own strength, they also have the option of decreasing that of their opponents. Several of these maneuvers reflect the opposite side of the negotiators' own strength maneuvers. Specifically, instead of developing their own outside options, negotiators can maneuver to deny or close off the options of their opponents. For example, if the New York Yankees were attempting to trade a hard-hitting outfielder to the

Kansas City Royals, they no doubt would find that the Royals were simultaneously negotiating with one or two other teams for their sluggers. To weaken the Royals, the Yankees also could open negotiations for these same sluggers or purchase them and thereby reduce the Royals' options.

Instead of closing off some of the opponents' options, negotiators can choose to weaken opponents by preventing them from forming coalitions against negotiators. The facets of these maneuvers closely parallel those used by negotiators to form coalitions against opponents: Negotiators can bribe the potential members of the opponents' coalitions to ensure that they do not bond with the opponents. Negotiators can threaten them, negotiate with them, or use any of their available power bases to deny opponents their coalitions, allies, or assistants.

If opponents already possess allies, negotiators can undertake maneuvers to isolate the opponents within these ranks. A very good example of this maneuver is the Soviet Union's actions of March 1969. At this time the Soviets, via the Warsaw Pact, formally proposed to the North Atlantic Treaty Organization (NATO) a conference on European security. The Soviets had previously prescribed an all-European conference and knew that many of the U.S. allies—specifically, Italy, France, West Germany, and Great Britain—would be eager to accept this proposal and that the United States would strongly oppose it. Therefore, the Soviet leadership proposed the conference, knowing that the United States would reject it and hoping that the United States thus would find itself isolated within NATO (Kissinger, 1979).

In addition to closing off the opponents' alternatives, and preventing opponents from forming their own coalitions, negotiators can maneuver to weaken their opponents' stands within their own constituencies. Although maneuvers of this sort do reduce opponents' strength, they also bring with them considerable risks. Opponents finding themselves out of sync with their constituencies on the one hand might become recalcitrant or belligerent with negotiators in order to prove themselves. On the other hand, the opponents might consider themselves independent of their constituencies and thereby become an unpredictable loose cannon in the negotiation, or they might simply become combative because they resent the negotiators' incursions into their home waters.

A similar and inadvisable weakening maneuver is to disorganize the opponent's constituency. Such a maneuver is undertaken at times to underpin the "divide and conquer" strategy, yet it can result in a constituency too disorganized to negotiate. As the reader might recall, the disorganization of the Iranian constituency frequently thwarted U.S.

attempts to negotiate the return of the hostages. As one senior Western diplomat noted during the last months of 1980, "The Iranians were too disorganized before the U.S. elections. A crucial deadline was missed, and now we're in for further haggling. It's a bit of a hangover" ("An Offer," 1980).

To reduce the opponent's strength, negotiators can attempt to reduce the opponent's status or perceived expertise. Negotiators can challenge the opponent's credibility or reduce the opponent's holdings of bargaining chips. Finally, a simple, but subtle and effective, maneuver is to recruit an opponent's close associate to assist in a negotiation. In 1980 presidential candidate Ronald Reagan used such a maneuver in his negotiation with Gerald Ford to make him "superdirector" vice-president. During the Republican Convention, Henry Kissinger called on the Reagan people to discuss his upcoming speech. The conversation quickly turned to Ford as Reagan's running mate, and one Reagan aide requested that Kissinger ask Ford to consider the tap. Later that evening, Ford sought Kissinger's counsel on the proposition, and Kissinger supported the Reagan proposal. Kissinger went on to make his convention speech, with the Reagan forces reinforcing his cooperation by passing word on the convention floor that he was not to be booed (Alpern, 1980).

Leveraging the Opponent

In addition to increasing their own strength and reducing that of their opponents, negotiators can attempt a third type of maneuver: leveraging the opponent. As opposed to the aforementioned maneuvers, leveraging does not alter the relative strength of the negotiator. These maneuvers involve movements that bring the negotiators' strengths to bear at a time or place that is to their advantage and to the disadvantage of the opponents (that is, flanking maneuvers).

Some think that only weak negotiators need maneuver in this fashion, because strong negotiators can lead from strength, bringing their strength to bear successfully at either the opponents' weak or strong points. However, consider the 250-pound mugger who attempted to lead from strength in attacking a proverbial 120-pound weakling who had only a yellow belt in Tae Kwon-Do. As the attacker closed upon the victim, the latter simply stepped aside, kicked, and broke the assailant's knee. The point should be clear: even the strong have their weak points, and they need to maneuver to protect them.

This example illustrates the first leverage maneuver: movement to address the opponent's weak point or to protect the negotiator's own points of weakness. On occasion this maneuver might be as simple as waiting for the situation in which the opponent is most vulnerable. For example, a union negotiator might withhold a number of complaints until management becomes involved in a negotiation with one or more other unions. The union negotiator knows that in such a situation the management is more malleable: it fears that a lack of agreement with the first union, along with its visible wildcat strikes and slowdowns, might precipitate recalcitrance on the part of the other unions as they close ranks behind the first or as they seek to demonstrate their own toughness.

Before attempting to address the opponent's weak points, the negotiator can research exhaustively to determine where the opponent is vulnerable and how her strong points relate to her weak. At times the negotiator might find that the opponent's strengths are independent of her weaknesses; at other times, the strong positions might be underpinned with weak ones. Consider as an illustration a settlement negotiation between the defendant's and plaintiff's attorneys. The former, after considerable effort, obtains evidence (for example, a document) that compromises the testimony of a plaintiff witness. The defendant's attorney now has located a point at which the plaintiff's case is flawed and thus can concentrate on that point in an attempt to reduce the amount sought by the plaintiff. However, the defendant's attorney had better first determine the relationship of the witness's testimony to the rest of the case. If the witness's testimony is simply corroborative, the attorney has found a weak point that provides only slight leverage. In contrast, if the testimony is pivotal to the plaintiff's case—for example, it establishes that the plaintiff was in no way at fault—the compromising evidence proffers considerable leverage.

At this point it is worth noting that the negotiator's establishment of the opportunity to address the opponent's weak point is a maneuver. Exercise of the leverage, failure to address the point, and threats to exploit the weakness are tactics. More specifically, the maneuver sets up or underpins the tactic, whereas the tactic is the implementation of the course of action made possible by the maneuver. To clarify this distinction, let us continue with the legal example. The defendant's attorney has improved her position—a maneuver—by obtaining a document that can provide leverage in her negotiation with the plaintiff's attorney. She can use it in the negotiation by revealing the document before the judge who is overseeing the settlement—a coercive tactic—and thereby exert considerable leverage against the opponent. In contrast, the defendant's attorney can adopt a threat tactic, stating that she has a document that compromises the plaintiff's witness and weakens the plaintiff's case; therefore, if the plaintiff's attorney does not reduce her demands by a certain amount, the attorney holding the document will display it in the settlement proceeding and in any subsequent trial.

A maneuver similar to addressing the opponent's weak point is the end run. Here the negotiator, after encountering resistance in the negotiation with the opponent, shifts ploys—logic, arguments, threats, bribes, power plays, and so on—to another party, usually a different person in the opponent's bargaining team or the opponent's constituency. This maneuver, which is frequently employed—for example, by children who pull an end run to Dad when the negotiation with Mom develops into a quarrel—is to be distinguished from a flanking maneuver. The end run typically avoids the opponent; the negotiator circles around the opponent to another party. In contrast, the flanking maneuver concentrates upon the opponent, seeking to set up an attack on the opponent's weak side.

Defensive Maneuvers

The previously described maneuvers are by nature offensive in that they underpin offensive tactics or strategies for the negotiators. At times, however, negotiators find themselves on the defense and must maneuver to enhance their positions there. The most frequently employed defensive maneuver is stepping aside without attacking whenever the opponent leads from strength. As Peters (1955) notes, negotiators faced with a demand they cannot refuse may ask to set the issue aside for the time being. Doing so allows negotiators to avoid the capitulation that would result if they did not maneuver and thereby lets them save face and gives them time before the issue is addressed once again.

At times, stepping aside on a weak issue is not possible, and negotiators find they must instead step or fall back. An axiom of battle quoted from the time of Sun Tse states that commanders must always leave a line of retreat for their opponents. It is also wise to develop one for yourself. The development of a fallback position has disadvantages as well as advantages.

On the negative side, planning for this maneuver erodes the tenacity with which a negotiator's former position is maintained. More specifically, the availability of a fallback position enhances the probability of using it. Perhaps more important, as Kissinger (1979) notes, once a fallback position exists in formal negotiations—no matter how qualified—it eventually will be put forward to the opponent, first by private comments or press leaks and later as a formal proposal. Corroboration for Kissinger's observation is embarrassingly clear in U.S. Secretary of State Cyrus Vance's abortive attempt to open strategic arms talks with the Soviets in 1977. Vance had an opening position and a fallback. In Moscow he presented first the former, which was rejected, and the latter, which also was rejected; he then was subjected to a moderate browbeating and sent home with no counterproposals (Steele, 1977). Why such crisp and rapid *nyets* from the Soviets? It seems that earlier, in the United States, Vance had informed Soviet Ambassador Anatoly Dobrynin of the United States' opening position and for some unknown reason also revealed what the backup position would be. Thus, Dobrynin no doubt cabled both to Moscow, allowing the Soviet leadership to have an impressive package of rejections waiting for Vance.

On the positive side, a negotiator's fallback can be significantly useful if it is undertaken when necessary and if it unfolds according to a plan. All negotiators at times find themselves at a disadvantage on some issue or in some negotiation and thus must concede. Such encounters are very common: The inflation rate is skyrocketing, so the management representative must give a large raise to a powerful union. For a newspaper, the city beat is becoming more complex, forcing the senior managing editor to hire more reporters. Because nurses in a neighboring hospital are receiving child care services, a hospital administrator must be responsive to such demands made by staff nurses. Failure to retreat under such circumstances can prove quite costly; many of us can recall instances in which a negotiator did not "roll with the punch," or "retreat and regroup." One negotiator took and lost a strike in a negotiation that would have cost her less if she had conceded. Another failed to concede on a valid point raised by a subordinate and thereby lost a valued employee. Still another clung tenaciously to a minor point, lost a major sale to a potential customer, and appeared a fool to his boss.

When the fallback position becomes necessary and is undertaken, it should be guided with a plan. As in warfare, the plan for a fallback or retrograde maneuver is the most difficult of all maneuvers to devise and implement. In its simplest form, the plan for the "advance to the rear" has two facets: the backup goal and the route or routes to the goal. Once the negotiator has determined that holding to her original goal or demands is proving too costly (for example, it risks a low CL_{alt} of not settling), she begins to concede—moving back toward the fallback position—along the chosen route (the one in which she incurs the least costs). If she cannot hold or obtain agreement at the primary fallback position, she then may move back to the secondary one and continue this process until she concludes that any further retreat will drive her NO below her CL_{alt}. At this point, she should break off the negotiations.

In sifting through the examples of retrograde maneuvers to be found in legal, managerial, union-management, marketing, and international negotiations, we find most often that negotiators attempt to cover their retreats with the smokescreen of threatening tactics. They bark as they back. A classic example of this was seen in April of 1981, when President Reagan fell back and lifted the embargo on grain sales to the Soviet Union. He and his secretary of state, Alexander Haig, did not wish to lift the embargo, but it was an issue he had to fall back on. Reagan had made a campaign promise to lift the embargo, and farmers were pressuring him to concede. Thus, he fell back but covered his retreat; the day following the announcement of the embargo termination, Haig threatened that the United States would effect an "across-the-board" embargo on goods to the Soviet Union if the Soviet Union invaded Poland.

Summary

This chapter developed an overview and taxonomy for negotiation maneuvers. Most are employed for offensive purposes and include ploys to increase the negotiator's strength, decrease the opponent's strength, and underpin subsequent leverage of the opponent. In addition to the offensive maneuvers, there are those of defense, in which the negotiator attempts to improve upon a vulnerable position. Whether offensive or defensive, the negotiator's maneuvers are intended to support his or her tactics—endeavors to achieve the negotiation goals.

The next chapter focuses on the negotiator's tactics, and Chapter 5 offers guidance on the manner in which they are to be meshed into effective strategies.

Chapter 4

Negotiation Tactics

● As noted previously, negotiation tactics are the components of the strategy or the facets of the broad plan used to obtain the desired outcomes from a negotiation. The tactics are the most salient aspects of a negotiation and form multiple labyrinths for the investigator probing into the negotiation process. When attempting to travel these passages, we become aware of an apparent inconsistency: the different tactics are manifold—there are perhaps two hundred—and yet the negotiation literature pays them only a passing nod. When they are discussed, tactics are confused with maneuvers or strategies. At times they are distinguished from, but curtly subordinated to, strategies, with definitions such as "tactics are the components of a negotiation strategy." They are simplified, are usually reduced to a single tough-soft continuum, and in no source are treated in detail. Unfortunately, such oversights and shortcuts mask the complexity of the negotiation process and detract from the appreciation and understanding of its core components.

To better appreciate the complexity of negotiation tactics, take about fifteen minutes to record the various tactics you have used, encountered, or observed in your day-to-day bargaining. After a few minutes you no doubt will accumulate a lengthy list. Some of the tactics will be nice and some, not so nice; some will be rational and others, emotional; some will be persuasive and others, blunt. No doubt you also will surmise that your appreciation for the richness of tactics has degenerated into confusion.

Categories of Negotiation Tactics

Although confusion is the initial response, after some reflection an order can be perceived. One of the first distinctions that can be drawn among the tactics is that of rational versus irrational tactics (Exhibit 4–1). Most tactics are rational; negotiators engage in these behaviors to modify those of their opponents. That is, they persuade, threaten, reward, cheat, scare, and reward opponents in a manner the opponents understand and in so doing appear rational themselves. In contrast, some tactics do not appear rational. For example, a negotiator abruptly changes his or her mind and breaks off a negotiation even when the opponent is conceding rather generously. One party makes an irrelevant outburst. Another says, "Give me $10,000 (tax free), or I'll kill myself."

Within the rational category lie most of the negotiation tactics, which can be grouped into two principal subcategories: debate and bargaining tactics. Debate tactics are those in which the parties engage in discussions, explications, interpretations, syntheses, and proposals to decide jointly upon an agreement that is acceptable to both sides. Bargaining tactics, in contrast, encompass negotiator (opponent) behaviors that are intended to move, direct, or constrain the opponent (negotiator).

The bargaining tactics can be further divided into the aggressive, nonaggressive, and posturing tactics. The aggressive tactics include announced intentions to harm the opponent if he or she does not engage in the desired behavior (threat tactics) and the specific attempts to inflict such harm (coercive tactics). The nonaggressive tactics include those that are conciliatory (that is, ones that gain the opponent's good will and eventual compliance through a number of affable acts). Also in the nonaggressive category are those tactics that reward the opponent.

In the far right branch of Exhibit 4–1 are the posturing tactics, moves by the negotiator that are intended to portray the negotiator as tough, soft, or neutral. Although aggressive tactics, no doubt, portray the negotiator as a tough negotiator, and the nonaggressive tactics make the negotiator appear relatively soft, they must be considered different from posturing tactics such as stares, expressed diffidence,

Exhibit 4-1. Negotiation Tactics.

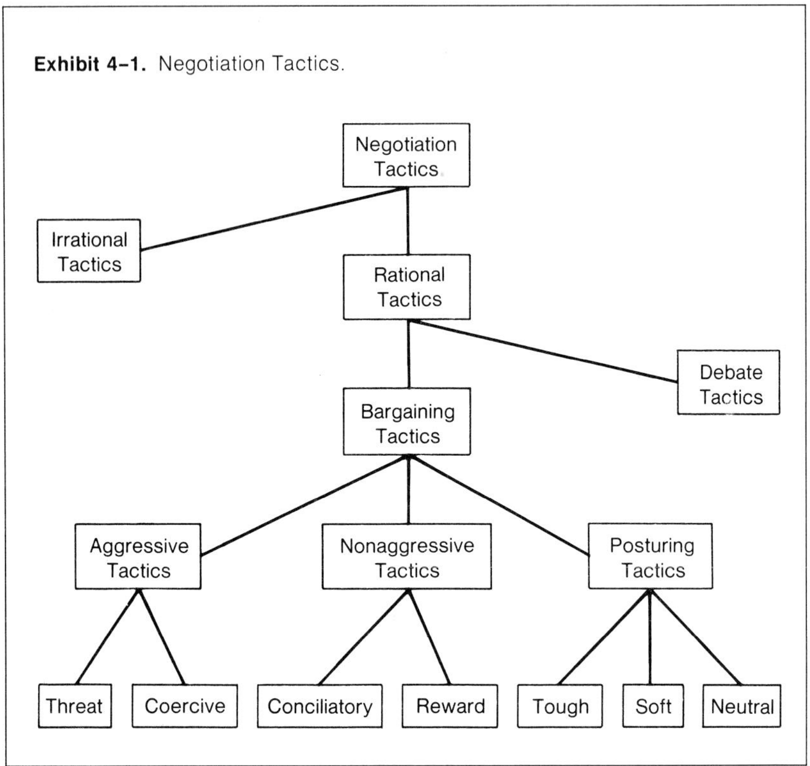

and displayed patience, which are intended primarily to create an image of the negotiator that will, in turn, alter the opponent's behavior.

We now turn from a general overview of the negotiation tactics to a more detailed look at each of the categories. We will investigate first the bargaining tactics; then those of debate; and, finally, the controversial irrational tactics.

Aggressive Bargaining Tactics

Threat Tactics

Deutsch (1973), Sawyer and Guetzkow (1965), Schelling (1960), and others have defined a *threat* as the expressed intention to engage in behavior that is detrimental to one's opponent, if the opponent does not engage or fails to engage in the prescribed behavior. Such a definition fits our perceptions of a *threat* and requires little expansion to formulate the definition for threat tactics: the negotiator's expressed indication that harm will befall the opponent if the latter fails to behave in the prescribed manner.

The threat tactics (Exhibit 4–2) can be viewed as compellent versus deterrent, mands versus tacts, and overt versus tacit. Schelling's (1960) discussion limns the distinction between compellent and deterrent tactics. Compellent tactics require that the opponent behave in a certain manner in order to avoid the negotiator's coercive act. In contrast, deterrent tactics (for example, a "trip wire") dictate that the opponent not engage in a particular behavior. As Tedeschi and Bonoma (1977) note, tactics that entail a compellent threat are more often perceived as aggressive or hostile, because the opponent facing them must engage in the prescribed behavior and forgo all others. Conversely, deterrent tactics forbid only one behavior and thereby allow the opponent to engage in all others.

Mands include those tactics—real or sham—in which the negotiator controls the consequences. For example, during the Iranian hostage negotiations, the Iranians continually threatened to put the hostages on trial if the United States did not make the prescribed concession ("An Answer," 1980). In this case, the Iranians did control the consequences: they could put the hostages on trial. Likewise, a labor union, when it threatens to employ a slowdown, is using a mand. A lawyer in a settlement negotiation also is using a mand in threatening to take a case to trial if the opposing lawyer does not settle on a specific sum.

As opposed to mands, the negotiator may use *tacts* (warnings) on the opponent. In this case, the negotiator's tactics specify the contingencies, as do the mands; however, the consequences in this case remain beyond the control of the negotiator. A salary negotiation between a manager and a white-collar employee provides a suitable distinction between the two tactics. The manager who threatens to fire a subordinate if she does not take a wage cut would be employing a mand. In contrast, a manager is employing tact when she informs an employee that his failure to absorb a wage cut will lead his peers to follow suit and thereby bankrupt the company.

Finally, the distinction between the overtly and tacitly (implied) threatening tactics is intuitively clear. The overt tactics (for example, commitment) are manifest and open to view, whereas the tacit tactics (for example, a show of force in a side area) are more subtle and unspoken.

Exhibit 4–2. Aggressive Bargaining Tactics.

Threat tactics

- Ask for commitment
- Use "trip wire"
- Show force in side area
- Use overkill in one negotiation facet
- Claim opponent abuse to hint retaliation
- Claim opponent abuse and specify retaliation
- Claim opponent irrationality and hint retaliation
- Hint about declining patience
- Make claims of tension production
- Make claims of opponent's deliberate misunderstanding
- Claim opponent is dragging feet

Coercive tactics

- Slightly punitive
  - Imply concession by voicing complaint
  - Refuse to disclose intentions or goals
  - Refuse to answer question
  - Exaggerate impatience
- Somewhat punitive
  - Cause delays
  - Withhold information
  - Demand commitment from opponent
  - Make reasonable proposal when aware it will be rejected
  - Behave inconsistently
  - Make "salami concessions" (make very many small concessions)
  - Demonstrate that breaking off negotiations would be costly
- Moderately punitive
  - Demand that opponent make first offer
  - Sequence advantageously on agenda items
  - Overplay own hand
  - Up the ante
  - Exhaust opponent
- Very punitive
  - Demand goals prior to and as condition of negotiation
  - Set extreme position and dredge up compromise
  - Extract concessions for those one intended to make
  - Reduce opponent's self-image
  - Concede on a straw issue and then demand reciprocity
  - Break communications
  - Give tangible sanctions
  - Deadlock
  - Use personal abuse
- Extremely punitive
  - Open negotiation with test of strength
  - Demand what opponent cannot give
  - Escalate demands to prevent agreement
  - "Wring the rag dry"
  - Fail to adhere to agreement

Coercive Tactics

Whereas the threat tactics specify forthcoming aversive outcomes, the coercive bargaining tactics inflict them upon the opponent, remove positive outcomes, or block the opponent's acquisition of positive outcomes. Numbering about forty or so, these tactics can be sorted according to punitiveness into five categories: slightly, somewhat, moderately, very, or extremely punitive. The slightly punitive tactics listed in Exhibit 4–2 are for the most part passive. They do not assist the opponent in any way. They put the opponent on the defensive–for example, exaggerated impatience. They block the opponent's progress, but they do not remove positive outcomes or inflict aversive ones.

The somewhat punitive tactics are more active. They not only place opponents on the defensive; they also block their progress. For example, withholding relevant information can block or restrain an opponent's movement toward goals. This tactic at one time was employed quite frequently in legal negotiations before being recognized as a punitive negotiation tactic, and it was eliminated with a "discovery" procedure. In pretrial negotiations of civil cases today, the judge will allow discovery by the two attorneys. That is, each attorney may ask the opposing attorney, that attorney's clients, and third parties questions designed to provide information relevant to the case. People queried are placed under oath and thereby are required to answer the questions truthfully. If they do not wish to answer a question, they must petition the judge for permission not to answer. Discovery also allows the attorneys access to documents possessed by the opponent, and it can even include permission to enter the opponent's premises. Although discovery does not obligate an opposing attorney to provide all information he or she feels is relevant to the case under negotiation, it does preclude this attorney from withholding any information the other attorney considers relevant.

Most of the moderately punitive tactics are self-explanatory; however, perhaps the second—sequencing advantageously on agenda items—would profit from explication. Here the negotiator sets the agenda so that the items of importance to her are negotiated first. If the opponent accepts such a sequencing, she thereby admits her weakness, because such a protocol is to her disadvantage. Once the negotiation unfolds, this agenda is quite costly, because the negotiator will quickly ascertain whether or not she is to obtain what she wants in the exchange. If she is obtaining a favorable package, she will continue the negotiation; if not, she will abandon it or charge the opponent a high price for her continued participation. The opponent, however, cannot operate with such flexibility in this agenda, because the items of interest to her are raised late in the negotiation.

The very punitive tactics reveal options that appear to entail risks for the negotiator employing them. Such a conclusion is valid, since the risk to the negotiator in employing the punitive tactics—like the risk to one employing any weapon—increases with the potency of the tactic. One of these tactics—a ploy typically used in the international realm by the stronger of two nations who are at war—entails demanding a concession from the opponent prior to and as a condition of negotiation. In such a case, the stronger nation concludes that a negotiation risks the relinquishment of some advantage that it possesses on the battlefield or in some other arena; therefore, it feels that demanding concessions up front is valid, even if punitive. Such a tactic is not found only in the international realm. Many a marriage counselor—professional or ad hoc—has encountered a spouse who, when coaxed to discuss the difficulties, replied, "There's nothing to talk about." In most cases like this, the spouse is tacitly asking for a concession from the counterpart as a condition for participation in a discussion. Plaintiff's attorneys also commonly use this tactic when they initially approach the defendant. The plaintiff has a suit and plans to take it to trial. When the defendant or the defendant's attorney asks about settling the case out of court (that is, opening a negotiation to do so), the plaintiff's attorney will quickly demand some concession (for example, an admission of liability) as a condition for opening the settlement negotiation.

The extremely punitive tactics include those that not only remove and block opponents' acquisitions of positive outcomes; they also inflict aversive outcomes upon opponents. Such tactics can prove quite risky, even though they are not saliently so. Consider, for instance, "wringing the rag dry" (Peters, 1955). With this tactic, the negotiator seizes every possible advantage and never gives up on an issue—major or minor—until the possibilities of gaining it have been exhausted. As Kissinger (1979) notes, such a tactic is not without its high costs. In using this tactic, negotiators overreach themselves, fail to capitalize on opportunities, and inadvertently weaken their own positions:

> Sometimes Gromyko's tactics left a bad taste. Occasionally he—or those who made the political decisions—overreached themselves. The absolute refusal to take any chance, the desire to squeeze every possible gain from a negotiation caused, as I have already shown, the Soviet leaders to miss the opportunity for a summit in 1970 when our bargaining position was weak, or in 1971 before our announcement of the Peking summit. Had the Soviets responded in 1970, they would at

least have complicated our China initiative and inhibited our freedom of maneuver in the Middle East. Had the Kremlin ended its cat-and-mouse game about the summit in the spring of 1971 and announced a date, its bargaining position would have been greatly strengthened. (Kissinger, 1979, p. 791)

An unethical extension of the "wringing the rag dry" or "ratchet" tactic is the opponent's failure to adhere to the negotiated agreement. Such postagreement backpedaling is most salient in high-level, important agreements. For example, in 1980 the Polish government was allegedly guilty of using this tactic continually after its agreements with the Solidarity Union. The government would readily agree to implement changes, raise pay, and shorten the workweek in order to end worker strikes. After the strikes ended, however, the government again would sack the current government head and fail to honor parts of the agreement.

Nonaggressive Bargaining Tactics

The nonaggressive bargaining tactics are divided into two categories: conciliatory and reward. Conciliatory tactics are those that attempt to improve the affective relationship with the opponent, and reward tactics are those that follow preferred opponent behavior so as to increase the probability of its continuance.

Conciliatory Tactics

Negotiators and opponents operate on a number of planes in their exchanges, two of which are the affective and the logical. On the logical plane, opponents negotiate as they do because it maximizes their objective payoffs; for example, they make a concession because they feel it will be reciprocated. On the affective plane, however, opponents' behavior is determined by a variety of more subjective factors, and it is to the negotiators' benefit at times to adopt tactics that improve the interaction on this level. Some of the most effective of these tactics are those that win the opponents' trust. The first ten tactics in Exhibit 4–3 serve this function. Some of these—for example, expressing guilt—are of low cost to the negotiators. Others—for example, "stopping the clock" when continued running would be beneficial (Brecher, 1980)—are quite costly. As costly as these tactics may be, negotiators at times must adopt them in order to elevate their

Exhibit 4–3. Nonaggressive Bargaining Tactics.

Conciliatory tactics

- Invite opponent's inspection
- Reveal one's goals or objectives
- Impose a deadline on self
- Stop the clock
- Render self vulnerable to opponent
- Express guilt
- Use language similar to opponent's
- Define common problems
- Express common dislikes
- Criticize self
- Apologize
- Banter with opponent
- Emphasize similarities with opponent
- Build friendship with opponent
- Flatter opponent
- Exhibit patience with opponent
- Put forth position devised by opponent
- Use empty posturing
- Make an offer opponent can refuse
- "Fire an empty cannon"
- "Handle the hot potato"
- Make first concession
- Volunteer concession
- Concede at deadlock
- Give concession that requires no reciprocity
- Give concession that cannot be reciprocated
- Retract a demand
- Do not call for an expected concession
- Fail to retaliate
- Attack common enemy
- Debase an original demand
- Announce forthcoming moves
- Make goals, strategy, tactics, and maneuvers plain to opponent
- Negotiate consistently, cooperatively, or competitively
- Deny threats were intended
- Justify threats or coercive tactics
- Explain why one's goals must remain secret
- Signal or clarify shifts in bargaining style

Reward tactics

- Make concessions
- Use systematic, reliable concession making
- Make concession that later cannot be delivered
- Complain about opponent's toughness
- Raise straw issues in order to lose them

Exhibit 4–3. Nonaggressive Bargaining Tactics (continued).

Reward tactics (continued)

- Make concessions early in negotiation
- Provide opponent with line of retreat
- Arrange for third party to suggest concession
- Imply, after opponent's concession, that concession was minor one
- Use opened communications
- Make early commitments
- Display trust in opponent
- Enable opponent to revise commitments
- Confer status on opponent
- Compliment opponent on ideas, presentation, and so on
- Express appreciation for opponent's behavior

opponents' trust to useful levels or to overcome distrust generated by past threats, coercive moves, conflicts, irrational tactics, or insults.

To improve other affective ties with opponents, negotiators can banter with them to put them at ease and emphasize the similarity between their backgrounds, tastes, socks, heights, noses, and so on. Over time, negotiators can simply attempt to build a friendship with opponents (Tedeschi & Bonoma, 1977; Tedeschi, Bonoma, & Novinson, 1970).

Likewise, negotiators can flatter their opponents—both privately and publicly—and, having bequeathed the opponents this positive reputation, later call upon them to uphold it. In almost every negotiation we can observe negotiators and opponents commenting on the positive attributes of the other, but few of us are privy to the latter facet of this tactic. Kissinger (1979) provides an amusing subtle example of giving the opponent a reputation to uphold. In September 1969 Golda Meir made her first trip to Washington as Israeli prime minister to meet with President Richard Nixon. At that time, Nixon's feelings toward Jewish people were ambivalent; he favored a strong Israel, but Jews had not strongly supported him in or out of the White House. Knowing full well Nixon's ambivalence, Meir hailed him as "an old friend of the Jewish people," a comment that shocked many, but one that gave Nixon a reputation to uphold. It is debatable whether Nixon supported Israel so strongly in the next few years in order to uphold his reputation or in order to serve the U.S. national interest. However, few feel that Meir's flattery was in vain.

Patience with the opponent no doubt helps build a positive relationship, as does spontaneously putting forth a proposition devised by the opponent. Likewise, empty posturing—putting up a straw front of toughness so that the opponent can call the bluff—improves the relationship. This last tactic is so effective because, in a sense, it serves as a gift to opponents. As it portrays them as tough bargainers, it allows them to gain face before themselves as well as before their peers.

Conferring gifts upon the opponent, such as making offers the opponent can refuse, "firing empty cannons," and "handling hot potatoes," similarly lubricates relations on the conciliatory level. So do the credit-building tactics, yet these entail more subtlety. Note that making the first concession banks considerable credits for the negotiator, as does the voluntary concession (that is, a concession that is not forced upon the negotiator nor is tacitly required by reciprocity). Like the first and voluntary concessions, a concession that breaks a deadlock also reaps blue chips, as does one that requires no reciprocity. As one example of the last type of concession, a negotiator can say, "OK, you've convinced me on that point." As a second example, Actress Carol Burnett's lawyers, in their pretrial sparring with the *National Enquirer,* dropped their suit from $10 million to about $2 million because the *National Enquirer's* lawyers convinced them to consider that the paper's profit was only $1 million per year.

In addition, debasing an original demand generates credits along a different avenue. Here negotiators follow an original demand with several new ones. These subsequent demands, by virtue of their numbers, tend to debase the currency and thereby reduce the perceived importance of the original demand.

While building credits with opponents, negotiators also demonstrate their reliability. They can announce their forthcoming moves (Osgood, 1959); likewise, they can make their goals, strategy, tactics, and maneuvers plain to opponents. In addition, negotiators can build a reliable image by being reliable—specifically, by being consistently cooperative or competitive. Consistent cooperativeness, no doubt, is preferred by opponents; however, they most often will opt for consistent competitiveness instead of more random behavior.

Reward Tactics

As noted earlier, reward tactics are those that follow preferred opponent behavior so as to increase the probability of its continuance. The most obvious of these is a negotiator's giving the opponent a salient reward—negotiator concession—immediately after the opponent concedes or behaves cooperatively. The initial concession, along with the negotiator's subsequent systematic and reliable concession making, serves as a powerful reinforcement to the opponent (Wall, 1977). At times a negotiator might even make concessions that cannot be delivered (Smith, 1980), setting up problems for the subsequent bargaining but reinforcing the opponent's desired response within the present negotiation.

After substantive concessions, the most valued reward the negotiator can hand the opponent is "face." Opponents require face before their subordinates, peers, constituents, and themselves (Pruitt & Johnson, 1970). By using the tactics delineated in Exhibit 4–3—from complaints about the opponent's toughness through the provision of a line of retreat—a negotiator can provide face before these parties.

In addition to using concessions and giving face, the negotiator can reinforce the opponent's behavior with promptness, open communications, early commitments, status, compliments, and other "gifts" of high valence to the opponent.

Posturing Bargaining Tactics

The last category of bargaining is the posturing tactics (Exhibit 4–4). Posturing is behavior undertaken to give appearances of strength, weakness, or neutrality to the opponent. Posturing tactics can include tactics found in any of the other categories. The distinction between a tactic when used for posturing and when used for such purposes as aggression, conciliation, irrationality, and debate is that a posturing tactic is one used principally to alter the opponent's perception of the negotiator—the type of person the negotiator is and his or her probable behavior—whereas the other tactics are used primarily to alter the opponent's behavior more directly.

Tough Posturing

The first posturing category, tough posturing, entails blunt, hostile behavior, as is exemplified by the first twelve tactics in Exhibit 4–4. Also included in this category are tactics that exhibit or project strength, but do so subtly, such as the preemptive concession. In making a preemptive concession the negotiator takes care to make a concession before an outside event or the opponent's action requires

Exhibit 4–4. Posturing Bargaining Tactics.

Tough posturing

- Express nondeference
- Boycott negotiation sessions
- Ignore opponent or mediator
- Deadlock
- Ignore deadlines
- Set deadlines
- Set deadlines and then ignore them
- Accept deadline and then remain entrenched as it approaches
- Surprise opponent
- Entrench self on minor issue
- Call opponent on a threat
- Reciprocate opponent delays
- Make preemptive concessions
- Recommend and then yield the preemptive concession

Soft posturing

- Express deference
- Observe deadlines
- Behave in friendly manner
- Use consistent, "nonsurprise" negotiation
- Appear vulnerable or unprepared
- Demonstrate inabilities
- Proffer poorly conceived proposals or demands
- Reveal lack of resources
- Fall back quickly from positions of proclaimed importance
- Appear malleable or inconsistent
- Alter demands
- Employ irrational points
- Hint at weak commitments

Neutral posturing

- Demonstrate patience
- Communicate nebulously
- Claim no authority to negotiate
- Claim outside reasons for lack of concessions

it. For example, if the negotiator knows that the opponent soon will demand a concession, the negotiator can make the concession before the demand has been laid on the table. Such accelerated concession making allows the negotiator to appear strong, even though he has conceded to an opponent. A clever version of the preemptive concession is for the negotiator, when he knows he inevitably will have to make a concession, to recommend the concession. With such a tactic, the negotiator gleans credit for the concession or his insight and concomitantly retains his staid reputation.

At the opposite end of the continuum, once the opponent has made a demand and the preemptive concession is thereby impossible, the negotiator often will endure enormous costs rather than concede. For example, Lech Walesa of the Polish Solidarity Union in 1981 repeatedly refused to make minor concessions to the Polish government, even though he was under intense pressure by the Soviet Union to make such concessions. Even though the cost of the concession is significantly less than the probable cost of not conceding, a negotiator may stand firm because capitulating, he feels, would portray him as a weak negotiator, an image that he does not relish and one that might cost him dearly in the future.

Soft Posturing

Soft posturing at times entails the use of tactics opposite those employed in tough posturing. The negotiator expresses deference with gestures, eye movements, dress, and facial expressions; likewise, he or she observes deadlines, is friendly, and makes no surprising moves. Why would a negotiator posture softly? The major explanation is that it can lead to reciprocal deference and cooperative synergistic exchanges with the opponent. Also, soft posturing at times can be used to set the opponent up for future exploitation.

Neutral Posturing

Instead of employing tough or soft posturing tactics, the negotiator can adopt neutral posturing tactics. As opposed to "no posturing," which entails the use of no tactics to imply toughness or softness, neutral posturing tactics imply that the negotiator is neither aggressive nor soft. In posturing neutrally, a negotiator can practice the fine art of being absolutely nebulous. Implementing a different tactic, he can claim he has no authority to negotiate, perhaps not wishing to waste his concessions when the opponent does not wish to negotiate. Likewise, he can claim outside reasons for the absence of concessions to or agreement with the opponent.

As an example of this last tactic, consider Gerald Ford's explanation of his reluctance to be Ronald Reagan's "superdirector" vice-presidential running mate. Ford stated that the arrangement would not work: There would be tensions between his and Reagan's staffs, and there would be much press criticism of Ford's changing his official residence to Michigan or Colorado to sidestep the difficulties posed by the Twelfth Amendment (Alpern, 1980). Although the neutral posturing tactics, listed in Exhibit 4–4, are not as salient or splashy as those of tough or soft posturing, many negotiators seem to prefer the neutral stance. Tough posturing usually is interpreted by the opponent as being somewhat hostile, and soft posturing tactics tempt the opponent to engage in some exploitative moves. As a golden mean, neutral posturing seems to avoid the hostile impression as well as the exploitative temptations, and therefore it is frequently adopted.

Debate Tactics

Having dealt with the aggressive, nonaggressive, and posturing bargaining tactics, we now turn to those of debate, which, in conjunction with the bargaining tactics, make up the rational negotiation tactics. This representation is consistent with the view held by Walcott, Hopmann, and King (1977), as well as others, that negotiations are in part "exercises in persuasive debate"—exercises that coexist with the bargaining processes. The topics debated and the methods by which they are debated interact and intermesh to produce an impressive number of debate tactics. Although they are numerous, the tactics can be comprehended easily by dividing them into three intuitively distinct categories: structural, joint–problem-solving, and competitive debates (Exhibit 4–5).

Structural Debates

Structural debates center upon personal relationships and the issues. Agreements are reached concerning the number of persons who will negotiate over the various issues and the authority that the opponent, constituents, mediators, arbitrators, and other third parties will have in the negotiation. For example, early in the negotiation the negotiator might demand that the opposing constituency send a person to the negotiation who has the authority to settle rather than one who is instructed to report back to the constituency (Mintzberg, 1973).

Like structuring the personal relations, structuring the issues frequently requires joint tactics or undertakings. One bargaining party cannot undertake tactics such as grouping issues, norm formation for the negotiation, rule setting, and codification of these norms and rules

Exhibit 4–5. Debate Tactics.

Structural debates

- Demand that opponent have authority to settle
- Discuss establishment of secret/dual channels
- Divide negotiator-opponent unit into smaller teams
- Hold informal conferences
- Avoid issues
- Fractionate issues
- Simplify issues
- Group issues
- Develop norms for negotiation
- Establish rules
- Intelligently neglect issues
- Agree on areas in which there is to be cooperation, competition, and conflict

Joint–problem-solving debates

- Make hypothetical offers
- "Think out loud" about potential opponent responses
- Make heuristic searches for solutions
- Use question-and-answer method
- Make preference orderings
- Use role reversal
- State other's position
- Float "trial balloon"
- Use "double-string balloon"

Competitive debates

- Make proposals and explications
- Provide information consistent with proposal
- Use persuasion
- Use logic
- Address direct questions to "less coached" member of opponent's team
- Accuse opponent to elicit revealing responses
- Bait opponent
- Deliberately misrepresent information
- Make large number of proposals
- Communicate misinformation

(Midgaard & Underdal, 1977) on her own. Similarly, the negotiator and opponent must jointly limit the areas of disagreement, partake in intelligent neglect of some issues, decide the arenas in which they will cooperate, and break combative cycles into manageable parts.

Joint–Problem-solving Debates

Joint problem solving entails attempts to eliminate misunderstanding between the negotiator and opponent, to improve communication, and to align perceptions of reality. Although the problem solving is labeled *joint,* some of the tactics falling into this category can be undertaken independently as well as jointly. Most of these techniques, listed in Exhibit 4–5, are quite clear, perhaps with the exception of heuristic searches, role reversal, and "double-string balloons." In the heuristic search, the negotiator and opponent frequently vary their proposals and, through a process of trial and error, search for options that are acceptable to both (Pruitt & Lewis, 1977). The offers and counteroffers here are not hypothetical; the two parties are expected to close on any offer accepted by the opponent. However, any offer, in a sense, is voided whenever the opponent makes a counterproposal.

In the role reversal process the negotiator and opponent present and defend the viewpoint of the other in the negotiations (Johnson, 1967). This procedure increases the objective understanding of the other's position and enhances the perceived similarity of each negotiator's position.

To implement the "double-string balloon" tactic, the negotiator first "floats a trial balloon." Specifically, she announces or has leaked by a third party or someone of low rank in her constituency that her side plans to take a certain step. As this balloon is released, a senior constituent or the negotiator herself holds a second string. If the opponent's or a third party's reaction is highly unfavorable, the senior party will retract the balloon (that is, disavow the idea).

Competitive Debates

The final debate category is one of competition. In this realm the debates are undertaken by the negotiator to improve her own position, to undermine that of the opponent, or both. Most frequently, the negotiator makes her proposals, explicates them, and provides information consistent with her proposals and explications. She attempts to persuade the opponent and third parties, seeking to align their views with hers. Similarly, the negotiator can present a crystal-clear logic for her opponent's concessions and provide outsider corroboration for these arguments. To accompany her logic, demands, and corroboration, the negotiator can engage in varied influence attempts, seeking to enhance her referent, expert, and legitimate power (Rubin & Brown, 1975). She can camouflage her own preferences and utilities by offering a large number of proposals to the opponent (Dunlop & Healy, 1955).

Irrational Tactics

The discussion of the debate tactics closes the coverage of the rational negotiation tactics and furnishes a nice juxtaposition for the second set of negotiation tactics, the irrational ones. What are irrational tactics? The response is best gleaned from the definition of *rational decision making.* Decision makers are considered to be rational if they choose alternatives that, given their current expectations and preferences, provide higher NOs than the alternatives not chosen. Given this definition, irrational negotiation tactics (Exhibit 4–6) will be considered those undertaken by negotiators that seemingly provide them with NOs that are lower than those provided by alternative behaviors.

From this grafted definition blooms the logical question, Why would such a tactic be undertaken? One retort comes from Carl Sagan (1980), astronomer and philosopher, who notes the following in his discussion of Cold War tactics:

> Truly effective nuclear bluffing, however, includes occasional postures of irrationality, or distancing from the horrors of nuclear war. Then the potential enemy is tempted to submit on points of dispute rather than unleash a global confrontation which the aura of irrationality has made possible. (p. 326)

This short paragraph contains a convincing reason for employing irrationality: it aids a threat tactic. The United States' threat to deliver a massive nuclear strike to the Soviet Union if the latter invades West Germany, has little credibility in and of itself. Such an act is not rational, because its NO–the prestige the United States gains or the face it saves *minus* the cost of a nuclear strike in its heartland—definitely has a debit balance. However, this threat does appear credible if the United States can appear irrational, and the ultimate technique for appearing irrational is to be irrational. Thus, an irrational move such as delivering a nuclear strike on Iran would greatly enhance the efficacy of the threat to the Soviets.

A second reason for employing irrational tactics is more defensive. Only rational behavior is subject to threats and coercion. Therefore, the negotiator who can be or can appear to be irrational cannot be successfully threatened, blackmailed, or deterred (Ellsberg, 1975).

Exhibit 4–6. Irrational Tactics.

Invite devastating opponent retaliation
Appear irrational by being irrational
Fail to capitulate to a costly opponent threat
Guarantee low future outcomes to self
Sever high outcome options
Escalate own losses
Draw opponent into a debilitating cycle
Level an emotional outburst at opponent
Speak impulsively or carelessly
Argue illogically
Abruptly change own mind
Use "calculated incompetence"

Negotiators also engage in irrational moves for emotional reasons; for instance, they hate the opponent, feel hurt, wish to retaliate, envy the opponent's position, and so on. When applied for this reason or any other, the irrational tactics also provide an ancillary function; they confuse the opponent, buying time for the negotiator to maneuver advantageously and to employ additional tactics.

As for the specific irrational tactics, the primary one perhaps is obvious by now: negotiators can engage in behavior that provides them with a loss or a relatively low NO. For instance, surgeons can refuse to operate if they do not have an operating room scheduled for the time they want. Likewise, a negotiator can take steps that ensure low NOs in the future, as does the newspaper reporter who quits because her story was pulled from the front page. Or negotiators can deny themselves high payoff options, as does the army that burns its bridges, the hijacker who shoots his hostage, or the striking union that destroys the company's machines.

In addition, negotiators can heighten their apparent and actual irrationality by taking steps that increasingly enhance their present and future losses or that further reduce their outside options. To harm the opponents as well as themselves, negotiators can seduce their opponents into increasing their own losses and in turn find themselves drawn further into the escalation by opponents. Negotiators can level an irrational emotional outburst at opponents, which usually sets them back. Negotiators can be impulsively and impressively careless in what they say, the logic they pursue, the concessions they offer, the demands they make, and so on. Instead of being careless, negotiators might abruptly change their minds, as Egyptian President Anwar el-Sadat did when he threw the Soviets out of Egypt in 1972. Negotiators can make a proposal, retract it, and then fire off a second one in which they suddenly reverse themselves. Finally, they can exhibit "calculated incompetence" (Walton & McKersie, 1965), selecting a representative or composing a bargaining team that does not understand the payoffs of the alternatives under negotiation.

Summary

This chapter has examined the tactics open to negotiators pursuing bargaining goals and, it is hoped, has convinced the reader that the category of behavior labeled *tactics* encompasses a plethora of actions that can be applied individually or woven together into complex labyrinths. No doubt this discussion has simultaneously generated questions about which tactics should be used, how they should be combined, and the contingencies under which the individual tactics and combinations can be employed effectively. The subsequent chapter addresses these inquiries.

Chapter 5

Negotiation Strategies

● As a negotiation draws near, negotiators are impatient to get on with it, and many do so without sufficient reflection upon the course they will pursue. In the unfolding negotiation, they apply a strategy that has served them well in the past or adopt an amalgam of tactics that seem appropriate. An observer of several of these negotiators wonders why they fare as well as they do. After some deliberation, the answer surfaces: the opponent is equally unsophisticated.

Why follow a strategy in a negotiation? Because tactics are more effective when fitted together in a synergistic plan. What strategy should be formulated in a negotiation? The answer to this question is best introduced by an example. Return for a minute to the U.S. Pacific strategy in World War II. The commanders first decided upon a goal—the offensive engagement and destruction of Japan. With this goal, as well as the situational constraints and opportunities, in mind, they closed upon a strategy (the double pincer), with the separate claws of the pincer delegated to MacArthur and Nimitz. In the western pincer, MacArthur used a strategy that moved the Japanese out of the route he was assigned by addressing weak, as opposed to strong, islands. Note that MacArthur started with a goal (movement north along a western route) and closed upon a strategy that used a method (island hopping) to serve a strategic function (movement or elimination of the enemy from the chosen route).

So it should be with a negotiation strategy: the negotiator should concentrate on goals, functions, and methods. By combining several elements of the previous discussion, we find that the formulation of a negotiation strategy is a surmountable challenge; as noted in Chapter 1, the goal of negotiators in exchanges with opponents is a high

NO—one that is above their CL and CL_{alt}. Later, using the Edgeworth Box, it was argued that negotiators raise their NOs by (1) moving the opponents to give high NOs, (2) directing the opponents, and (3) constraining them.

How does the negotiator move, direct, and constrain the opponent? That is, what methods are used to accomplish these three strategic functions? The answer is *tactics.* As Chapter 1 noted, opponents' behavior in negotiations is determined in part by their NO, CL, and CL_{alt}. By using tactics, negotiators can modify these and thereby strategically move, direct, and constrain opponents.

Exhibit 5–1 illustrates this in a matrix with the strategic functions (moving, directing, and constraining the opponent) arranged along the horizontal axis, and the methods serving these functions (alteration of the opponent's NO, CL, and CL_{alt}) arranged along the vertical axis. As Chapter 4 noted, the negotiator's tactics can be used to raise *or* lower the opponent's NO, CL, and CL_{alt}; therefore, each of the strategic methods is divided into two classes, with the result being NO↑, NO↓, CL↑, CL↓, CL_{alt}↑, and CL_{alt}↓.

Within the body of the resultant matrix, then, can be arranged the tactics that move, direct, and constrain the opponent by raising or lowering his or her NO, CL, or CL_{alt}. Specifically, the conciliatory and reward tactics move, direct, and constrain the opponent by raising his or her NO. In contrast, the threat and coercive tactics fulfill these functions by lowering the opponent's NO. The soft posturing tactics alter the opponent's behavior through raising the CL; the tough posturing and competitive debate tactics, by lowering the opponent's CL, move, direct, and constrain the opponent. Finally, the competitive debate, threat, and coercive tactics constrain the opponent by lowering his or her CL_{alt}.

There also are vacant cells within the matrix. Of these, the CL↑/constrain cell is unfilled because raising the opponent's CL does not constrain him or her; it has the opposite effect. Likewise, the four lower left cells are vacant because alterations of the opponent's CL_{alt} do not move or direct the opponent within the negotiation. Finally, because raising the opponent's CL_{alt} will reduce, as opposed to induce, constraints, the CL_{alt}↑/ constrain cell also is empty.

Four tactical sets have not been included in the matrix—neutral posturing, structural debates, joint-problem-solving debates, and irra-

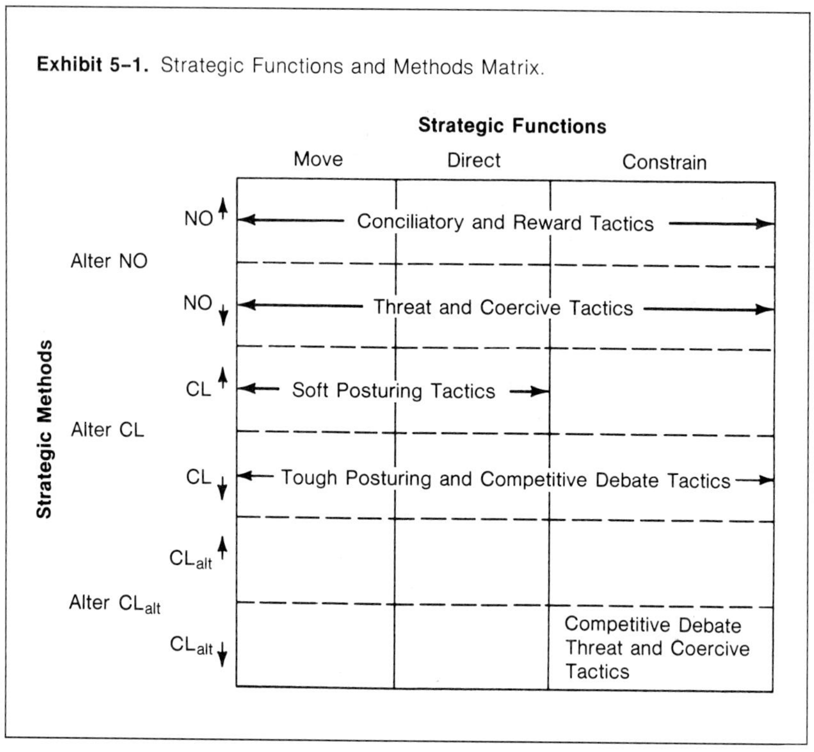

Strategic Functions
Move
Direct
Constrain
Strategic Methods
Alter NO
NO ↑
Conciliatory and Reward Tactics
NO ↓
Threat and Coercive Tactics
Alter CL
CL ↑
Soft Posturing Tactics
CL ↓
Tough Posturing and Competitive Debate Tactics
Alter CLalt
CLalt ↑
CLalt ↓
Competitive Debate
Threat and Coercive
Tactics

Exhibit 5–1. Strategic Functions and Methods Matrix.

tional tactics. Omission of the first three sets is based on the premise that the tactics contained within them are useful in almost all negotiations; therefore, the negotiator should not devote time and resources to probes of their contingent effectiveness. The irrational tactics have been omitted because they should never be used; by definition, the costs from their use exceed the gains. It might be argued that at times the negotiator might wish to appear irrational so as to make some gain. This is a weak argument for retaining irrational tactics in the inventory, because, as Hermann Kahn notes, the pretense of irrationality is not reliable. People must intend to be irrational to provide the legitimate appearance of irrationality. If this be the case, it also seems that a negotiator's constituency seldom would want their negotiator cultivating irrationality and uncontrol in representing their interests.

Given that negotiators can use their tactics to move, direct, and constrain opponents, how do negotiators build these into a synergistic strategy? They develop a strategy in which, with a broad sweep, they eliminate inappropriate tactics and then combine the remaining viable tactics into a finely tuned strategy.

Negotiation Strategy Development[1]

As does any strategy development, the first step in the negotiation arena is the identification of the goal to be pursued. This goal will vary from negotiator to negotiator. It will be altered according to the situation and can change along with the opponent. Some negotiators, for example, may wish to destroy their opponents; others, to make them look good. Many negotiators wish to obtain high NOs for themselves, and others prefer to keep their constituents' interests paramount. The list could continue for pages, yet the point is now salient. The first step for negotiators is the establishment of goals; then they must pursue them in the negotiation.

For exemplary purposes, assume that the negotiator's goals are twofold. The first goal is the attainment of high NOs from the negotiation; second is the goal of establishing the proper stage for any subsequent negotiation. This latter goal might be considered one of seeking a high future NO or, as Fisher and Ury (1981) present it, seeking a preservation of the negotiator-opponent relationship.

Decision Rules

Having established the goals, or criteria, for sorting among the tactics, the negotiator now develops rules or diagnostic questions that ensure that these goals will be met or protected. In developing these rules, the negotiator's objective is not to close immediately upon "the" correct tactics. Rather, it is first to eliminate tactics that do not serve that goal in a particular situation.

The following pages first present sets of decision rules that protect the chosen goals (high NOs and acceptable future relationship/ NO); each set protects these goals by calling for the elimination of tactics whenever they do not facilitate the tandem objectives. Following this discussion are some proposals for combining the remaining tactics into an effective strategy.

---

[1]The following section draws heavily on Vroom and Yetton's (1973) development of leadership prescriptions.

Rules to Protect the Negotiator's NO

Elimination of Conciliatory and Reward Tactics • The first rule calling for the elimination of the conciliatory and reward tactics is that they be eliminated from the feasible set whenever the elasticity between the opponent's and negotiator's NOs is less than 1. In such a case, the returns to the negotiator (in terms of opponent movement, direction, and constraint) are less than the costs, and thus such sets of tactics should be abandoned.

A second factor to consider is the negotiator's power. If it is greater than that of the opponent, its use is preferable to devoting resources toward improving the relationship with the opponent or rewards for the opponent. This is because power is cheaper to use in most cases and thereby better protects the high NO for the negotiator.

Turning to bargainers' resources, negotiators should forgo any attempts to reward and conciliate opponents if their own resources are low. The logic for this proposition is straightforward. In a low-resource position, negotiators might find themselves stranded without resources—interpersonal as well as material—if they attempt to use them on opponents. Even if their resources are not depleted, negotiators with limited resources are likely to find that the investment of their scarce resources into moving, directing, and constraining opponents will have high utility costs to themselves.

Negotiators should not use conciliatory and reward tactics if their utility to opponents is low. For example, if an opponent's NO already were very high or if it were approximately equal to his or her CL, the marginal utility of additional outcomes would be low and thereby would have limited leverage against the opponent.

Finally, negotiators should not use conciliatory or reward tactics if the results or the process of applying them alienates their constituents, because such alienation can result in high immediate and long-run costs for negotiators. For example, negotiators might banter with opponents, build a friendship with them, or openly display their trust. Observing these tactics, negotiators' constituents would start to distrust them, question whose side they were representing, and take corrective actions such as highly structured directives, demotion, or replacement.

Elimination of Threat and Coercive Tactics • Negotiators should not use threat and coercive tactics if opponents have the power to retaliate and thereby lower the negotiators' NOs. In such a case, these tactics would quickly spawn a reduction in the negotiators' own NOs.

The same proscription—no threats or coercion—is appropriate whenever the tactics would drive an opponent's NO below the CL_{alt}, rendering the opponent independent of the negotiation. In such a case, the opponent would abandon the negotiation or impose high costs upon the negotiator for remaining.

A final rule for eliminating threat and coercive tactics is to eschew them whenever the opponent is engaging in appropriate behavior. When appropriate behavior (correct movement or constraint) occurs, it should be rewarded (that is, NO↑) instead of extinguished or punished. Initially, this might appear a trivial recommendation, yet it is violated all too frequently by negotiators who are attempting to maximize opponent concessions. For instance, in many negotiations, opponents will tender concessions only to be met with negotiator complaints, threats, and delays. Having been punished for engaging in this amicable behavior, the opponents' behavior—like any behavior following punishment—becomes highly variant: they may repeat their tender, withdraw the offer, attack, or do nothing.

Elimination of Soft Posturing Tactics • Turning to the tactics for altering the CL, we can quickly dispense with the soft posturing tactics—which raise the opponent's CL—by offering the general proposition that they, in almost all cases, should be eliminated. In some cases (for example, highly integrative situations), a raised opponent CL would be to the negotiator's benefit. However, most frequently a high CL will induce the opponent to raise his or her NO.

Elimination of Tough Posturing and Competitive Debate Tactics • In most cases negotiators should attempt to use tough posturing tactics along with those of competitive debate to lower the opponent's CL. There are two exceptions. First, if opponent dissatisfaction is to a negotiator's advantage, the tough posturing and competitive debate tactics should be eliminated from the feasible set. Recall that the difference between the opponent's CL and NO (CL > NO) roughly corresponds to the opponent's dissatisfaction level. In some cases this dissatisfaction leads opponents to overplay their hands, abandon favorable positions, agree hastily, and so on, and thus it works to the negotiator's favor. To allow and capitalize on these responses, negotiators should avoid any tough posturing and competitive debates.

A second rule for eliminating the tough posturing and competitive debate tactics focuses on cost: if these tactics are highly costly to the negotiator, they should be scrapped. At present, research on the value of reducing the opponent's CL is somewhat equivocal. At times it seems to work, and sometimes it fails to raise the NOs of negotiators employing it. Thus, for negotiators to incur a certain reduction in their NOs for a CL reduction that yields uncertain results seems inadvisable.

As can be noted in the lower right corner of Exhibit 5–1, competitive debate tactics, along with those of threat and coercion, can be used to constrain opponents by lowering their CL_{alt}. Whenever feasible, these tactics should be employed for this purpose, for an opponent with ample alternatives to agreement and negotiation no doubt will use these as leverage against the negotiator. However, they should not be employed whenever the opponent is already highly constrained. If the opponent possesses very few options outside the negotiation, any further constraint will be perceived quite negatively. Most likely, the result will be uncooperative, if not belligerent, behavior and thereby a reduced NO for the negotiator.

Rules to Protect the Negotiator's Future NO

Having delineated several rules to protect the negotiator's NO, we now turn to the development of some rules to ensure that the future relationship and negotiation with the opponent will prove fruitful.

Elimination of Conciliatory and Reward Tactics • A general rule for the elimination of the conciliatory and reward tactics is that they should be removed from the feasible set whenever the opponent is engaging in behavior that the negotiator does not wish to continue in the future. In such circumstances these tactics, along with those of the joint–problem-solving debate, reinforce such behavior, and increase the probability of its future occurrence.

Elimination of Threat and Coercive Tactics • Threat and coercive tactics should be discarded under three conditions. First, they must be removed from the negotiation set if the future relationship/negotiation is quite important. The logical underpinning for this rule is as follows: If these tactics prove successful in the current negotiation, the opponent probably will adjust to reduce their effectiveness in the next negotiation. If they do not prove successful in the first negotiation (for example, if the negotiator threatened unsuccessfully or did not back up a threat), they probably will also be of no value in the second.

Second, the threat and coercive tactics should be avoided if the opponent's CL_{alt} is high. In such a case, threatening and coercing opponents will not foster appropriate movement or constraint on their parts. Instead, it will engender their abandonment of the negotiation.

Finally, threats and coercion of opponents should be avoided if the ploys will be deleterious to the opponents' relationships with their constituents. In the long run, damaging opponents' relationships with their constituents spawns severe repercussions for negotiators. Not only will opponents retaliate, seeking to lower the negotiators' outcomes within future negotiations, they also will seek to undermine the negotiator-constituency relationship, and they moreover will explore all ploys for getting even with the negotiators.

Elimination of Soft Posturing Tactics • As the previous section noted, negotiators in almost all cases should avoid soft posturing. Some exceptions include occasions in which negotiators desire their opponents to overplay their hands or overly extend and thereby make themselves vulnerable to the negotiators' moves.

If there is to be a second negotiation, these exceptions are eliminated. That is, if a subsequent negotiation or the continuation of an affable negotiator-opponent relationship is desirable, soft posturing tactics are to be discarded.

Elimination of Tough Posturing and Competitive Debate Tactics • Tough posturing and competitive debate tactics should be eliminated whenever high joint outcomes will facilitate future relations. In such a case, a moderate level of aspiration for opponents will induce them to cooperate with negotiators in order to raise their own, as well as the others', NOs. If negotiators leveled their opponents' aspirations with tough posturing or competitive debates, such actions might thwart their efforts, reduce the shared high payoffs, and thereby dampen future relationships.

Second, these tactics should not be undertaken if the negotiation is highly visible to the opponent's constituency or is being observed by important third parties. In such cases, opponents will resent the threats to their NOs as well as to their reputations and will retaliate to save face and attain high NOs in both the present and future negotiations.

Finally, turning to the $CL_{alt}\downarrow$/constrain corner of the Exhibit 5–1 matrix, it seems inadvisable to use competitive debates, threats, and coercion to lower opponents' alternatives—thereby restraining them—whenever there is to be a second negotiation. To constrain opponents within the first negotiation will motivate them to acquire sufficient alternatives before the next negotiation. In addition, funneling an opponent into a negotiation via reduction of alternatives produces a less positive relationship than does effecting an agreement through conciliation and rewards.

Recapitulation

To this point in our formulation of a negotiation strategy we have noted that a negotiator can use a variety of tactics to alter the opponent's NO, CL, or CL_{alt} and thereby move, direct, and constrain the opponent. Given these opportunities, the negotiator, to be strategically effective, must first select goals—we chose high negotiator NO and preservation of the negotiator-opponent relationship. Second, the negotiator must deduce rules from logic, observations, or intuition that will eliminate ineffective tactics and thereby protect the selected goals. Having generated the rules, the negotiator then applies them to the bargaining situation, eliminates tactics, and from the remaining tactics devises a goal-oriented negotiation strategy.

Since the manner in which the negotiator uses the rules differs somewhat between simple and complex situations, we will first examine their use in a simple context. We then will turn to the complex situations and discuss weaving the tactics into a negotiation strategy.

Strategy Development: Simple Negotiation

For exemplary purposes, a previous section developed more than a dozen rules for eliminating tactics. A negotiator facing a complex important negotiation should develop and apply such an extensive set of rules. In contrast, prior to a somewhat simple encounter, a negotiator should develop and implement a more limited number in order to keep the costs of preparing for the negotiation below the probable NOs accruing from it.

Consider the rule development you, as a negotiator, would employ when facing a rather simple negotiation. Assume that you adhere to the tandem goals of (1) a high NO and (2) an amicable future relationship, and that your rule development proceeds roughly along the lines of the previous logic. You might argue as follows.

Protection of NOs

If my opponent is currently engaging in behavior that provides me with low NOs, I should not use conciliatory, reward, or soft posturing tactics. To employ these would reinforce the opponent's behavior and increase the probability of its future occurrence.

I, as a negotiator, also should consider the opponent's responses to my behavior. If my opponent is contingently cooperative (that is, is reciprocating my cooperative moves), I must override my previous rule somewhat and employ reward tactics. Although they risk reinforcement of inappropriate behavior, such tactics should prove effective by engendering the opponent's reciprocal cooperation. Additionally, under the expectation of contingent cooperation, I should discard debate, threats, coercion, and posturing in order to concentrate on the tactics that foster reciprocal cooperation—conciliation and reward.

If my opponent has abundant alternatives, I am cast into a weak bargaining position and should forgo the use of threats, coercion, and tough posturing. The use of such tactics will drive the opponent from the negotiation and agreement. In contrast, if my opponent possesses limited alternatives, I should lead from strength and use tactics other than soft posturing, neutral posturing, debate, or conciliation.

Protection of Future Relationship

If my future interaction/negotiation with my opponent is important, I must eliminate threat and coercive tactics from my feasible set. Although such tactics may prove fruitful in the current negotiation, my opponent no doubt will retaliate against them in the following interactions or at least will be somewhat alienated by them and devise mechanisms to neutralize their future effectiveness.

Rule Synthesis

In a simple negotiation, the limited number of rules can be combined into a decision tree delineating the negotiation tactics to be used under specific conditions (Exhibit 5–2). By moving from left to right along the tree, addressing each question at the top of the figure (for example, in this negotiation, is the opponent currently engaging in inappropriate behavior?), and then following the appropriate branch, the negotiator can close upon the tactical combination appropriate for the current negotiation.

Strategy Development: Complex Negotiation

Whereas the limited number of rules generated in a simple negotiation permits the use of a decision tree, the extensive number to be found in a complex negotiation results in a rather unwieldy tree. Therefore, as the rules exceed five—producing a possible thirty-two endpoints on the decision tree—it is more convenient to condense them into a tabular checklist.

Exhibit 5–3 condenses all the rules previously developed. It requires the negotiator, instead of following branches, to respond to the listed propositions with checks in the columns to the right of the

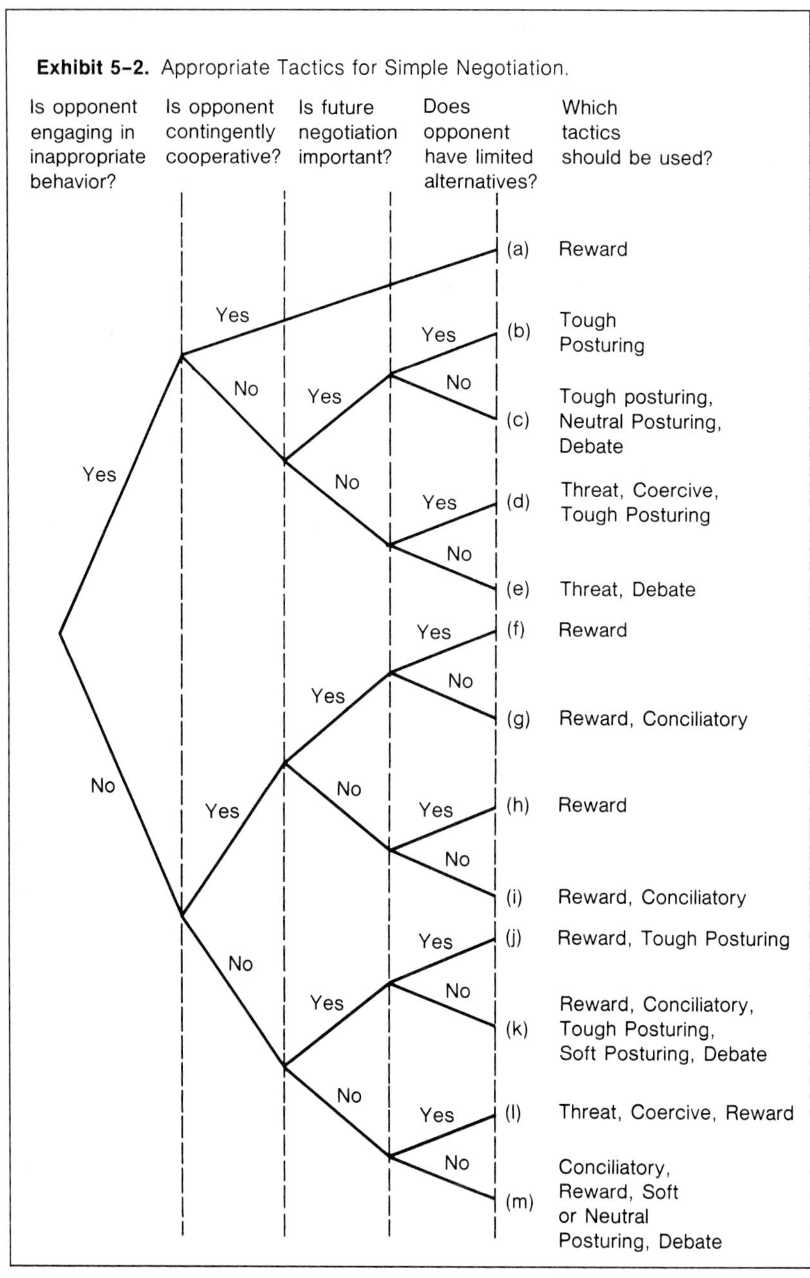

Exhibit 5–2. Appropriate Tactics for Simple Negotiation.

propositions. For example, in a given negotiation, the negotiator first asks if the elasticity between raising the opponent's NO (via conciliation and rewards) and increasing the negotiator's own NO is less than one. If the answer is affirmative—the opponent does not recipro-

Exhibit 5–3.
Rules for Elimination of Tactics.

	Check (✓) If Tactics Are to Be Eliminated						
	Conciliatory	Reward	Threat	Coercive	Soft Posturing	Tough Posturing	Competitive Debate
Rules to protect negotiator's NOs:							
1. Eliminate conciliatory and reward tactics if							
a. Elasticity between negotiator's costs and NOs is less than 1.	—	—					
b. Negotiator's power is greater than opponent's.	—	—					
c. Negotiator has few resources.	—	—					
d. Utility of negotiator's conciliations and rewards is low to opponent.	—	—					
e. Such tactics foster displeasure in negotiator's constituency.	—	—					
2. Eliminate threat and coercive tactics if							
a. Opponent's power is greater than negotiator's.			—	—			
b. NO↓ from threats and coercion makes opponent independent of the negotiation.			—	—			
c. Opponent is engaging in appropriate behavior.			—	—			
d. Opponent already is highly constrained.			—	—			
3. Eliminate tough posturing and competitive debate tactics if							
a. Opponent dissatisfaction is to negotiator's benefit.						—	—
b. These tactics are very costly to negotiator.						—	—
c. Opponent already is highly constrained. (Omit only competitive debate tactics.)							—
Rules to protect negotiator's future NOs:							
1. Eliminate conciliatory and reward tactics if opponent is engaging in inappropriate behavior.	—	—					
2. Eliminate threat and coercive tactics if							
a. Future negotiation/relationship is very important.			—	—			
b. Opponent's CL_{alt} is high.			—	—			
c. These tactics damage the opponent's relationship to his constituent.			—	—			
d. There is to be a second negotiation.			—	—			
3. Eliminate soft posturing in all but exceptional cases.					—		
4. Eliminate tough posturing and competitive debate tactics if							
a. High joint outcomes are important to future relations.						—	—
b. Negotiation is highly visible.						—	—
Total checks (eliminations) for each column	—	—	—	—	—	—	—
Divide by potential number of eliminations	6	6	8	8	1	4	5
Percentage	—	—	—	—	—	—	—

cate or judges the negotiator's concessions as demonstrations of weakness—the conciliatory and reward tactics are prime targets for elimination, and the negotiator checks the first two boxes to the right (that is, the boxes to eliminate conciliatory and reward tactics). If the answer is negative or the negotiator does not know the answer, the spaces are left blank. Having addressed each of the propositions, the negotiator then totals the number of checks in each column, converts these into percentages, and decides which tactics are to be eliminated. Then, from the remaining tactics, the negotiator formulates a general strategy.

There is a second advantage to using the table over the decision tree in planning complex negotiations. In a complex negotiation, the plethora of rules devised to protect the negotiator's goals usually will eliminate *all* the negotiation tactics. Thus, the negotiator must sort among the tactics on the basis of the relative, as opposed to absolute, merits of the tactics. For example, after applying all the rules in Exhibit 5–3, the negotiator might find he or she has votes *against* 60 percent of the conciliatory and reward criteria, 20 percent of the threat and coercive criteria, 50 percent of the soft posturing criteria, and 10 percent of the tough posturing and competitive debate criteria. Since the criteria in this case favor threat, coercive, tough posturing, and competitive debate tactics over conciliatory, reward, and soft posturing tactics, the negotiator would be well advised to develop a strategy meshing the tactics in the former set.

With Exhibit 5–3 as a guide in strategy formulation, consider as an example the development of a negotiation strategy by a mechanic who is approached by a customer. The day before, the mechanic had tuned the customer's—a local banker's—car. Today, a hot summer Saturday, the car develops trouble and has to be towed back to the shop. The customer is hot but pleasant; the tow cost $75; the customer's children are sweaty and hungry; and the mechanic finds a crack in the condenser he installed. Perhaps the crack was there when the condenser was installed, but maybe the crack formed when the engine heated. In either case, the mechanic can, if he wishes, change the condenser without the customer's knowledge and then find some other difficulty to correct.

The customer suggests that the mechanic fix the car immediately, pay the tow charge, and apologize. What strategy does the mechanic adopt? Assume that his goals are those previously delineated (high NO and preservation of the relationship); therefore, the propositions in Exhibit 5–3 are to be addressed. The appropriate responses are recorded in Exhibit 5–4.

Rules to Protect Mechanic's NO

1. a. Is the elasticity between the mechanic's costs and NOs less than 1?
Answer: Probably yes. The customer probably will not reciprocate concessions or make concessions that the mechanic can reward.
Action: Eliminate conciliatory and reward tactics.

b. Is the mechanic's power greater than the customer's?
Answer: No.
Action: No elimination.

c. Does the mechanic have limited resources?
Answer: No, he can supply what the customer demands.
Action: No elimination.

d. Is the marginal utility of rewards and conciliations low to the opponent?
Answer: No, the opponent values having her car repaired.
Action: No elimination.

e. Will the conciliations and rewards foster displeasure in the negotiator's constituency?
Answer: No, the constituency (the mechanic's wife and children) would like to have the customer treated well.
Action: No elimination.

2. a. Is the customer's power greater than that of the mechanic?
Answer: Yes, she holds the lease on the mechanic's garage.
Action: Eliminate the threat and coercive tactics.

b. Will NO↓ make the customer independent of the mechanic?
Answer: Yes. If the mechanic uses threats and coercive measures to reduce the customer's outcomes, the customer probably will see alternatives, such as suing the mechanic or going to another garage, as highly viable.
Action: Eliminate threat and coercive tactics.

c. Is the customer engaging in appropriate behavior that should be rewarded?
Answer: Yes, she is being very pleasant, given the conditions.
Action: Eliminate threat and coercive tactics.

d. Is the customer already highly constrained?
Answer: Yes, There are few other garages open on Saturday afternoon, and the cost of suing the mechanic would be high.
Action: Eliminate threat, coercive, and competitive debate tactics.

3. a. Is the customer's dissatisfaction to the mechanic's benefit?
Answer: No.

Action: No elimination.

b. Will the tough posturing and competitive debate tactics be costly to the mechanic?
Answer: No.
Action: No elimination.

Rules to Protect Future Relationship and NOs

1. Is the customer engaging in inappropriate behavior?
Answer: No.
Action: No elimination.

2. a. Is the future negotiation/relationship very important?
Answer: Yes. The customer has three cars and is a good customer.
Action: Eliminate threat and coercive tactics.

b. Is the customer's CL_{alt} high?
Answer: No.
Action: No elimination.

c. Will threat and coercive tactics damage the customer's relationship with her constituency?
Answer: Perhaps. Her husband is watching, and these tactics could make the customer appear incompetent to him.
Action: Eliminate threat and coercive tactics.

d. Is there to be a second negotiation?
Answer: Probably not.
Action: No elimination.

3. Is there some exception in this negotiation precluding the elimination of soft posturing tactics?
Answer: No.
Action: Eliminate soft posturing tactics.

4. a. Are high joint outcomes important to future relations?
Answer: No.
Action: No elimination.

b. Is the negotiation highly visible to constituents or others?
Answer: Yes.
Action: Eliminate tough posturing and competitive debate tactics.

Synthesis

Having addressed these questions and recorded the responses on Exhibit 5–4, we now can lay out the broad scope of the prescribed strategy. Of the six questions posed for eliminating the conciliatory and

Exhibit 5-4.
Practical Use of Rules for Elimination of Tactics.

Check (✓) If Tactics Are to Be Eliminated

	Conciliatory	Reward	Threat	Coercive	Soft Posturing	Tough Posturing	Competitive Debate
Rules to protect negotiator's NOs:							
1. Eliminate conciliatory and reward tactics if							
a. Elasticity between negotiator's costs and NOs is less than 1.	✓	✓					
b. Negotiator's power is greater than opponent's.	—	—					
c. Negotiator has few resources.	—	—					
d. Utility of negotiator's conciliations and rewards is low to opponent.	—	—					
e. Such tactics foster displeasure in negotiator's constituency.	—	—					
2. Eliminate threat and coercive tactics if							
a. Opponent's power is greater than negotiator's.			✓	✓			
b. NO↓ from threats and coercion makes opponent independent of the negotiation.			✓	✓			
c. Opponent is engaging in appropriate behavior.			✓	✓			
d. Opponent already is highly constrained.			✓	✓			
3. Eliminate tough posturing and competitive debate tactics if							
a. Opponent dissatisfaction is to negotiator's benefit.						—	—
b. These tactics are very costly to negotiator.						—	—
c. Opponent already is highly constrained. (Omit only competitive debate tactics.)							✓
Rules to protect negotiator's future NOs:							
1. Eliminate conciliatory and reward tactics if opponent is engaging in inappropriate behavior.	—	—					
2. Eliminate threat and coercive tactics if							
a. Future negotiation/relationship is very important.			✓	✓			
b. Opponent's CL_{alt} is high.			—	—			
c. These tactics damage the opponent's relationship to his constituent.			✓	✓			
d. There is to be a second negotiation.			—	—			
3. Eliminate soft posturing in all but exceptional cases.					✓		
4. Eliminate tough posturing and competitive debate tactics if							
a. High joint outcomes are important to future relations.						—	—
b. Negotiation is highly visible.						✓	✓
Total checks (eliminations) for each column	1	1	6	6	1	1	2
Divide by potential number of eliminations	6	6	8	8	1	4	5
Percentage	17	17	75	75	100	25	40

reward tactics, only one (17 percent) suggested they be eliminated as methods. However, 75 percent of the criteria for elimination of the threat tactics were affirmative; 75 percent called for elimination of the coercive tactics. The soft posturing tactics (100 percent) were also prime candidates for elimination. In contrast, the tough posturing tactics (25 percent of the questions favored elimination), along with those of competitive debate (40 percent of the questions favored elimination), survived the cut. In sum, the mechanic should use a combination of conciliatory, reward, tough posturing, and competitive debate tactics to move, direct, and constrain the customer. Since problem-solving debate is to be used unless a major criterion dictates its elimination, tactics from this category also will be judged viable.

The mechanic's task now becomes one of selecting the appropriate tactics from each of the targeted classes. After sifting through Exhibits 4–3, 4–4, and 4–5 in Chapter 4 to determine which tactics are relevant to or fit the current situation, the mechanic perhaps would close upon the tactics in Exhibit 5–5 as viable sets within each tactical class. (At this point it should be noted that the negotiator facing the simple negotiation, after using a decision tree and closing in upon the feasible sets of tactics, also must sort among the feasible tactics.)

With these tactics as the potential components of the overall strategy, the mechanic's task now becomes one of combining the selected tactics into a viable strategy. Here he must concentrate on the broad sweep rather than piece the tactics together in a potpourri. Recall that the task is to move, direct, and constrain the opponent by using tactics that lower her CL, raise her NO, and lower her CL_{alt}.

As a first cut, it seems logical that negotiators should lower their opponents' CL prior to raising their NO, because the reduction of the opponents' aspirations would make them more appreciative of the reward, conciliatory, and problem-solving orientation. Second, since opponents can abandon the negotiation, it appears advisable first to constrain them and then move and direct them. Combining these two ideas, a broad strategy surfaces: Initially, lower the opponent's CL with a strong emphasis on constraint. Subsequently, use conciliation, rewards, and problem solving to move and direct the opponent toward a suitable agreement.

Turning to specifics, the mechanic can open with an expression of nondeference, telling the customer that he is the expert on engines and he will determine where the fault lies. In the same breath, he can create a deadlock by telling the customer that the parts he installed are working perfectly. Having constrained the customer somewhat, the mechanic can look over the problem in detail and perhaps misrepresent some information; for example, he might note that the fuel filter

Exhibit 5-5. Selected Tactics.

Tactical Class	Viable Tactics
Conciliatory	Define common problem Apologize Attack common enemy Express common dislikes
Reward	Make concession Arrange for third party to suggest concession Provide opponent with line of retreat
Joint-problem-solving debate	Make hypothetical offers Use question-and-answer method State other's position
Tough posturing	Express nondeference Deadlock
Competitive debate	Make proposals and explications Use logic Use persuasion Deliberately misrepresent information

appears clogged or there is water in the gasoline. With the customer's aspirations in hand, he can ask some questions: Did the motor jerk violently before it stopped or just stop? Then he can define a common problem—new cars—saying, "Once you fix one thing on these new motors, another thing goes." He can attack a common enemy with a terse "They don't make them like they used to." He can apologize that he did not catch the fuel filter or water problem sooner.

Turning to reward tactics, he can make a concession if the customer is responding somewhat sympathetically. He can call over a third party (for example, an employee) to suggest joint concessions; for example, the mechanic will fix the car for the cost of parts only and will do so immediately. For her part, the customer will not ask the mechanic to pay the tow charge. Then the customer can be given a line of retreat with the suggestion that she take her car to the garage around the corner if she is not satisfied with this arrangement, or, if the customer wishes, she can obtain a second opinion. And the mechanic can replace the fuel filter at cost (and also the condenser, without mentioning the latter).

Strategy Development: A Recapitulation

In retrospect, consider the steps of a negotiation strategy development:

1. Choose the goals for the negotiation.
2. Develop rules or diagnostic questions that eliminate classes of tactics not serving these goals.
3. Condense the rules into an applicable format. On the one hand, if the negotiation is simple and the rules somewhat limited, a decision tree will prove useful. On the other hand, complex negotiations with a myriad of guiding rules will require condensing the rules into tabular form.
4. Investigate the negotiation situation, answer the questions posed in the decision tree or table, and conclude which tactical classes should be eliminated.
5. From the classes of tactics remaining, select the tactics that seem best suited to the negotiation situation.
6. Develop a broad plan that meshes and sequences the methods to be used (for example, NO↑, CL↓ and so on) and the functions to be served (move, direct, and constrain).
7. Weave the selected tactics together into the planned pursuits.

Our strategy development concentrated on the negotiation tactics to the exclusion of the maneuvers. How do these latter actions enter into the strategic picture? After selecting a tactic, negotiators must determine whether or not they have that tactic at their disposal. If they do not, they can discard it from their strategy or adopt maneuvers that facilitate its use. When choosing the latter avenue of attack, negotiators can sort among the maneuvers for those that underpin their tactic using a procedure somewhat analogous to the one just used for closing in upon the appropriate tactics.

Strategic Combinations

The mechanic-customer example called upon the negotiator to mesh and sequence the tactics of conciliation, reward, joint–problem-solving debate, tough posturing, and competitive debate into a viable strategy. As you contemplated this last stage of the strategy formulation, it no doubt became apparent that interfusing the selected tactics into a viable strategy is tricky. It often calls for negotiators' personal ingenuity and draws upon their special knowledge of the situation. To provide a catalyst for this ingenuity and complement the negotiator's expertise, the following sections offer some general road signs concerning the possible strategic combinations that can be formulated from sets of prescribed tactics.

Combination of Conciliatory, Reward, and Coercive Tactics

The negotiator who finds that a combination of conciliatory, reward, and coercive tactics is dictated by the situation can adopt a "blackmail" strategy. It is a very simple one in which the negotiator first engages in some maneuvers or tactics to raise the cost (lower the CL_{alt}) for not negotiating with her or for not meeting her subsequent demands. For example, she might take hostages; create or locate sensitive, compromising literature or photographs; and so on. Having secured her position, the negotiator usually directs the opponent with a clear demand and then raises the opponent's NO as the demands are met. As we have seen, the negotiator also can complement this tactical combination with threats that the opponent's NO will be reduced if she fails to comply with the demands.

Most people hearing about the blackmail strategy conjure up images of hijackers brandishing pistols and bank robbers holding hostages. However, this strategy most often is used in less colorful fashions within organizations. As time passes, certain persons within the organization intentionally or inadvertently flow into positions in which they become essential or critical factors in the organization's operation. In the skilled jobs they become the sole person who has the knowledge required to perform a certain task (for example, repair a complex or old machine). In managerial or middleman tasks, they delegate no responsibility, so they are the only people who know the correct or efficient manner in which to trace information, avoid red tape, comply with government regulations, or implement new decisions. Having generated a bottleneck position and located themselves in it, they tacitly or overtly bargain for what they want.

A second strategy combining the conciliatory, reward, and coercive tactics is the "retreat-and-flank" strategy. Although the negotiation literature does not report such a scheme, we can detect its elements in Lin Piao's battlefield ploys ("Tactical Concepts," 1951) and then draw from the available tactics to form an analogous negotiation strategy. Lin Piao notes that whenever the enemy attacks in force, the best response is to retreat and allow the enemy to extend itself. Having allowed the enemy to render itself vulnerable, the enemy should be flanked and struck at its most vulnerable point (Exhibit 5–6).

Exhibit 5–6. Lin Piao's Battle Strategy.

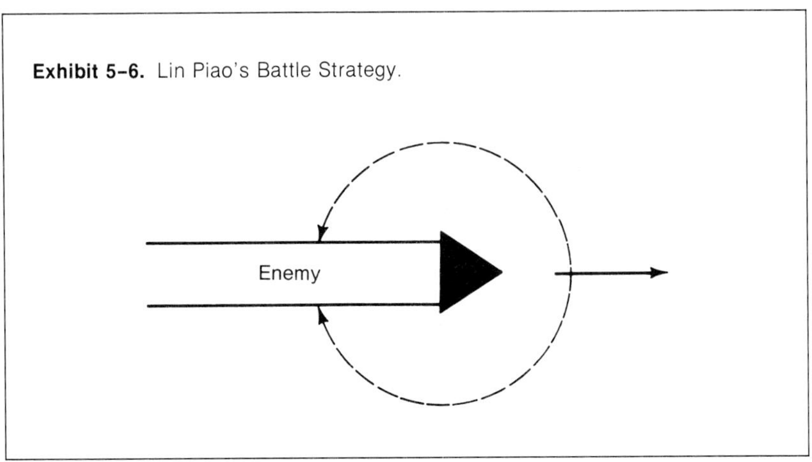

The development of a negotiation retreat-and-flank strategy requires that the negotiator allow the opponent, who is perhaps guided by a high CL, to advance and seize some short-run advantages in the negotiation. As the opponent advances and severs himself from some suitable alternatives, the negotiator can ingratiate himself and perhaps reward the advance with early concessions, complaints about the opponent's toughness, loss of straw issues, and so on. When the opponent is sufficiently vulnerable, the negotiator can turn the coercive tactics upon him and address his weak points with a high degree of leverage. As a variant of this strategy, if the opponent has extended his vulnerability sufficiently, the negotiator, instead of flanking and addressing a weak point, can attack the opponent head-on.

Both forms of the strategy often can be found employed within organizations. In a negotiation between two department heads (for example, production and marketing), the weaker (say, marketing), after making a few competitive overtures, will rapidly retreat on all fronts. The stronger, perceiving that she has the upper hand, will press forward and up her demands, as well as pound a table or two and tacitly threaten the weaker in front of others. Having allowed the stronger manager sufficient rope to hang herself, the weaker will pull an end run to a higher authority, citing evidence from the observers that the stronger needs to have her power reduced. Alternatively, and perhaps more likely, the weaker manager will form a coalition to control the stronger manager with the other managers who were present at the negotiation.

Combination of Conciliatory, Reward, Coercive, and Soft Posturing Tactics

The addition of soft posturing tactics to those previously discussed produces a strategy that can be dubbed the "decoy." With its roots probably embedded in goose hunting, the decoy strategy differs from the retreat and flank in that the opponent is enticed or decoyed into extending himself. To decoy the opponent, the negotiator engages in tactics to raise the opponent's CL—as German General Erwin Rommel's tanks in the African campaign enticed Allied tanks to chase them into the range of the Nazi antitank guns—so that the opponent will move to fulfill his raised aspirations. As the opponent does so, the negotiator cuts off or lowers the opponent's alternatives (with coercive tactics) and thereby raises the costs of not negotiating or agreeing with the negotiator. With a lowered CL_{alt} well secured, the negotiator then can successfully use conciliatory, reward, and even debate tactics to move, direct, and constrain the opponent.

Note that an advantage of the decoy strategy is that the negotiator need invest only limited resources in the conciliatory and reward tactics. This limited commitment is possible because the negotiator needs to raise the opponent's NOs very slightly. Even though the opponent might find himself dissatisfied ($CL > NO$), he still will agree or be malleable in negotiation, because his NOs do exceed his alternatives (that is, $NO > CL_{alt}$).

The decoy strategy can be somewhat complex, but the following simple example of its execution exhibits its major elements. Several years ago a group of Japanese migrant workers in California used this strategy quite effectively in negotiating with the growers. Their representative would approach a grower or number of small growers who were negotiating with other migrant crew chiefs and offer his crew's services for a price significantly below that of the other crews. The grower would accept and tell the other workers to seek employment elsewhere. After the competing workers were sufficiently distant—perhaps by a day or so—the Japanese would raise their prices. The growers, with ripe crops in the field and facing the alternative of having rotten crops, paid the price.

Occasionally the soft posturing portion of the decoy strategy can be replaced with a bluff, yielding a "bluff-twist" variant of the strategy. Here the negotiator initiates and accelerates the opponent's advance with a bluff that she knows the opponent will call. As the opponent calls the bluff and overextends herself, the negotiator cuts her alternatives and exploits the vulnerability.

In the early 1960s, the author witnessed a textile mill's use of this strategy in dealing with the union. The mill wanted the employees to strike so that it could fight and break the union; it thereby threatened to fire certain individuals if the union struck. Backed by its lawyers, the union knew that such firing could be successfully challenged in court, and they rose to the bait: they struck. The mill, having maneuvered well beforehand by squirreling away huge inventories, took the strike, did not fire the targeted persons, continued to supply customers, and broke the union.

Combination of Threat, Coercive, Tough Posturing, Competitive Debate, Conciliatory, and Reward Tactics

The concoction generated from the intermeshing of these tactics goes by several labels—tough/soft, black hat/white hat, and reformed sinner. It is based on the logic that an initial exposure to tough bargaining tactics renders the opponent more receptive to the negotiator's subsequent conciliations and rewards. More specifically, it is felt that the tough phase–threats, coercion, tough posturing, and competitive debate—"softens up" the opponent. Thereafter, the opponent is highly cognizant and appreciative of the negotiator's subsequent cooperation and quickly takes steps to reciprocate and reinforce such behavior. Pruitt and Kimmel (1977) offer a different, but similar, explanation for the effects of this strategy: "We assume that the initial phase of this kind of strategy produces an experience of mutual noncooperation which leads to insight into the value of mutual cooperation."

The logic underpinning this strategy seems theoretically, as well as intuitively, well grounded and is consistent with several real-world observations. For example, National Aeronautics and Space Administration (NASA) officials dealing with contractors typically use this strategy. One official (the tough, or black hat) first makes high demands of the contractor's negotiator or severely criticizes past performance. Subsequently, another NASA representative (the soft, or white hat) enters the bargaining to negotiate the specifics and final versions of the contract. Soviet negotiators are notorious for initially taking hard lines in negotiations and subsequently softening. Drill instructors in basic training camps employ the strategy with great delight, as do wiser and richer ticket scalpers. To improve the strategy, many scalpers work as male-female teams. The technique goes somewhat as follows. The male member will raise the tickets over his head outside the entrance to a sporting event, indicating that he has tickets for sale. Whenever he is approached by a potential buyer and asked his price, the scalper quotes a prearranged price, say, $8 each. When hearing this quote, his female counterpart retorts with surprise, "What? They're getting over $10 for them over there!" Hearing this, the male scalper, quickly developing a tacit compromise, says, "Oh well, guess I have to ask $9 for them, then." In labor negotiations, both the management and union constituencies don black hats and instruct their negotiators to be somewhat cooperative. And there is evidence to suggest that President Richard Nixon and Secretary of State Henry Kissinger used this strategy in negotiating with the North Vietnamese; Nixon would issue a strict warning, make high demands, or mine the harbors, and then Kissinger would enter the negotiation with a more conciliatory position.

A modification of this strategy entails the constituent's direction of threat, coercive, tough posturing, and competitive debate techniques toward the opponent's constituent. Simultaneously, the negotiator herself employs reward and conciliatory tactics. Such cooperation will be highly salient to the opponent and the opposing constituent, given the tough overtones of the negotiator's constituent. Thus, the opposing side—both opponent and constituent—will themselves be more likely to bargain cooperatively, because they will fear that the negotiator might become competitive (as they assume her constituent wishes).

Another possible variant of this potpourri is the negotiator's employment of such tactics as threats and coercion in unison with his constituent's use of conciliation and rewards. The author has witnessed one negotiation in which this strategy proved highly effective. In a labor negotiation, the management negotiator was taking a very hard line—but one he felt was reasonable—with the union negotiator over technological unemployment and was complementing it with ample threats and coercion. The union wanted no reduction in crew sizes. Claiming that the demand was for blatant featherbedding, the management negotiator wanted the crew size slashed by 50 percent. It became quite obvious to a third-party observer that a deadlock was soon to follow. It did. The union and management negotiators sparred for a couple of days, neither surrendering an inch from his position. Then, at the start of one session, the president of the company looked at his own negotiator and said he wanted to "talk turkey." He then looked at the opposing negotiator and said that he felt a reasonable agreement should be struck *now*. Thereupon he made one concession, and the opposing negotiator countered with a similar one. The constituent then said, "We are close to agreement; what should it be?" The opponent made another concession, and the president said, "Agreed."

If a negotiator wants to employ both facets of tough/soft strategy herself, she can pursue the "deadlock-and-concede" route. Here she first sets the agenda so that the issue of least importance to her is raised first; the most important, second; the second least important, third; the second most important, next, and so on. On the least important issue the negotiator deadlocks and concedes. Next, on the most important, she again reaches a deadlock, pressing the opponent to concede as a reciprocal gesture. In turn, the negotiator concedes on another unimportant item, attempting to continue a trend of conceding on unimportant items herself and pressuring the opponent to concede on important issues.

Reflections on Negotiation Strategy and Its Development

The procedure described in the previous section probably seems complex and time consuming. This is correct, yet the procedure can be defended. First, if the negotiation is simple, the negotiator should use a decision tree approach:

1. Choose goals for the negotiation.
2. Develop diagnostic questions that eliminate tactics not serving these goals.
3. Condense them into a simple decision tree.
4. Explore the negotiation environment, follow the appropriate tree branches, and close in upon the appropriate set of tactics.
5. Weave these into a goal-oriented, internally consistent strategy.

Second, we note that negotiations most often concern complex emotional and technical issues that fan out to affect and be affected by many other issues and events. Likewise, the number of potential strategies, given the over two hundred tactics available, is exceedingly large. Furthermore, the situational conditions, as we will note in the next chapter, are also highly variant.

Given these multiple sources of variety, it seems reasonable to devote considerable time and effort to the development of an optimal strategy. Unfortunately, there is an omnipresent temptation in negotiations—as in economics, management, construction, vacationing, motor repair, or teaching a child to swim—to forgo advance planning and then impose simple approaches upon complex problems. Very seldom are there simple solutions to complex problems, and to force a simple strategy upon a negotiation courts failure. Negotiators cannot simplify complex reality; instead, they must develop strategies that fit the situation.

A second Siren luring negotiators to ineffectiveness is the inviting ease of applying one strategy to all negotiations. This allurement must be shunned, because strategies in many situations prove less than effective. To support this proposition we will discuss four strategies—level of aspiration (LOA), reciprocity, reinforcement, and graduated reduction in tension (GRIT)—whose effectiveness have been examined. We will find that the effectiveness of each is, at best, contingent.

Level of Aspiration (LOA) Strategy

The LOA strategy (Siegel & Fouraker, 1960) holds that concessions by the negotiator raise the aspiration level (CL) of the opponent and thereby evoke his tough bargaining as he attempts to raise his NO to the CL. In contrast, low concessions (in terms of magnitude or frequency) reduce the opponent's CL and discourage him from negotiating toughly.

The strategist using this approach thus feels it pays to be tough, opening with a high demand, conceding little, and thereby driving the opponent's CL down. With a lowered CL, the opponent strives for less, settles for less, and is content with what he receives.

Does the LOA strategy work? Yukl's (1976) excellent review concludes that it is not always maximally effective. In considering the effects of the LOA strategy, he examines the effects of its separate facets: its hard (versus soft) initial offer, low (versus high) magnitude of concessions, and low (versus high) frequency of concessions. Yukl notes first the evidence as to the effect of the negotiator's initial offer: Chertkoff and Conley's (1967) study revealed that the negotiator's hard offer had no significant effect upon the opponent's offer or concessions. However, the tough initial offer did result in a more generous final offer by the opponent. In contrast, Yukl (1972b) himself found that when opponents were given some information about the negotiator's payoffs, the negotiator's initial offer produced no effect in either the subject's initial or final offer. When not informed about the negotiator's payoffs (Yukl, 1974a), the opponents were more affected by the negotiator's opening offer. The opponents encountering a hard initial offer made larger initial and final offers themselves. However, the amount of their overall concessions (initial offer minus final offer) was unaffected by the negotiator's initial offer.

As for the effects of low magnitude of negotiator concessions, the results again reveal that the strategy often is less than effective. Pruitt and Drews (1969) report that small negotiator concessions did not affect the opponent's final offer, yet Komorita and Brenner (1968) report that they do. The latter authors found that small negotiator concessions—specifically, hard contingent concessions (10 percent reciprocity)—produced the highest final offer, but only for opponents facing a high cost of delay. When no cost of delay existed, there was no effect from the negotiator's concessions.

With regard to the effects that the negotiator's small concessions have upon those of the opponent, Yukl (1972a, 1973, 1974a, 1974b), found support for the LOA strategy in four studies. Specifically, his results demonstrate that small (versus large) negotiator concessions yield higher opponent concessions. However, this effect did not appear under three circumstances: (1) when the negotiator's low concessions provided losses for the opponent (Yukl, 1973, 1974a); (2) when the negotiator, in addition to making small concessions, made very few concessions; and (3) when there was little payoff and the opponent knew the negotiator's payoffs (Yukl, 1974a).

Bartos (1967, 1970) also has investigated the effects of small concessions and has demonstrated that a low magnitude of concessions results in larger opponent concessions. Specifically, he usually found a negative correlation between the opponent's and negotiator's mean demands. However, when the relationship between the negotiator's concessions and profit was noted, the relationship was curvilinear; the moderate strategy was the most effective. Yukl (1976), in considering the data, points out the dilemma facing the negotiator using the LOA strategy: "Apparently, as a negotiator's toughness increased, he obtained greater concessions from the other negotiator but fewer agreements occurred. Since deadlocks resulted in zero profit, more than a moderate degree of toughness failed to produce any increase in the mean level of profits." Finally, Hamner's (1974) results tend to refute the LOA strategy. That is, he found that the opponent's concessions were lower, as were the negotiator's profits, whenever the negotiator pursued a hard strategy.

Whereas the evidence concerning the effects of the negotiator's hard initial offer and low concession magnitude are mixed but generally supportive of the LOA strategy, the data on the results from low frequency of concession are not. Both the studies by Chertkoff and Conley (1967) and Pruitt and Johnson (1970) show that the negotiator's frequency of concessions has no effect on the opponent's concessions.

Exhibit 5–7, which condenses the relevant studies cited by Yukl (1976) into chart form, shows the variable effectiveness of the LOA strategy. The strongest evidence seems to be that the negotiator's low initial offer and low magnitude of concessions result in more generous concessions by the opponent and a more favorable final offer. However, these results are limited to certain conditions, and the

Exhibit 5–7. Evidence for the LOA Strategy.

Negotiator's Behavior	Opponent's Resultant Behavior		
	Initial Offer	Final Offer	Concessions
Low Initial Offer	Chertkoff & Conley, 1967 (±)	Chertkoff & Conley, 1967 (+)	Chertkoff & Conley, 1967 (±)
	Yukl, 1972b (±)	Yukl, 1972b (±)	Yukl, 1974a (±)
	Yukl, 1974a (+)	Yukl, 1974a (+)	
Low Magnitude of Concessions		Pruitt & Drews, 1969 (±)	Yukl, 1972a. 1973, 1974a, 1974b (+)
		Komorita & Brenner, 1968 (+)	Hamner, 1974 (−)
		Komorita & Barnes, 1969 (+)	Bartos, 1967, 1970 (+ and ±)
Low Frequency of Concessions		Chertkoff & Conley, 1967 (±)	Chertkoff & Conley, 1967 (±)
		Pruitt & Johnson, 1970 (±)	Pruitt & Johnson, 1970 (±)

\+ Negotiator's behavior affects opponent's behavior in the manner predicted by the LOA theory.
± Negotiator's behavior has no effect on the opponent's behavior.
− Negotiator's behavior affects opponent's behavior oppositely from the LOA prediction.

Source: Based on G. A. Yukl (1976). *A review of laboratory research on two-party negotiation.* Unpublished manuscript, Baruch College, Wayne State University, Detroit.

payoffs from the strategy frequently are jeopardized by high frequency of deadlocks.

Reciprocity Strategy

Like the LOA strategy, the reciprocity strategy is effective only under certain conditions. This strategy is based on the reciprocity principle (Gouldner, 1960): people reciprocate the actions of others and expect others to reciprocate their behavior. As applied to the negotiation situation, this principle or hypothesis holds that negotiators (or opponents) expect their concessions to be reciprocated. If the concessions are reciprocated, they continue to make concessions; however, if opponents do not reciprocate, negotiators respond with few and small concessions. That is, they reciprocate, or retaliate against, the small concessions made by opponents.

The reciprocity strategy, therefore, is based on the assumption that tough negotiator moves—hard initial offers, low magnitude of concessions, and low frequency of concessions—will evoke tough opponent responses. Thus, it is considered preferable to make at least a moderate opening offer; to make large concessions to opponents in hopes that they will reciprocate; and to reciprocate for opponents' large concessions, so they will not retaliate for the violation of the reciprocity norm.

In the bargaining literature there is mixed support for the reciprocity strategy. The Chertkoff and Conley (1967) and Pruitt and Johnson (1970) studies found that opponents were willing to reciprocate the frequency of the negotiator's concessions, but not the magnitude. Likewise, Pruitt (1968) found that opponents reciprocated the frequency of concessions, and Esser and Komorita (1975) report that opponents made larger concessions whenever negotiators pursued a reciprocity strategy.

Additional references could be cited, but the general pattern would remain the same; support for the reciprocity strategy, like that for the LOA strategy, is mixed. In addition, the assumptions underpinning the two strategies are not supported in some situations. With regard to the LOA strategy, some studies have investigated the assumption that the negotiator's tough bargaining reduces the opponent's CL (Yukl, 1976). Dual measures of the CL measures were used: the opponent's "target"—that is, the highest expected settlement—and resistance point—that is, the minimally acceptable point (Walton & McKersie, 1965). Studies by Liebert, Smith, Hill, and Keiffer (1968) and Yukl (1974a) found that the opponent's resistance point was lowered by the negotiator's hard initial offer, but only when the negotiator's payoffs were unknown; however, Pruitt and Drews (1969) failed to find such a relationship. Yukl's (1974a, 1974b) two studies found opponents to have both lower target and resistance points whenever the negotiator made small concessions. Likewise, the studies by Druckman, Zechmeister, and Soloman (1972) and Rubin and Dimatteo (1972) found the opponent's CL reduced by tough negotiator bargaining. In contrast, Pruitt and Drews (1969) failed to find any relationship between the negotiator's bargaining and the opponent's CL.

Whereas the LOA strategy has mixed support from the literature, the reciprocity strategy has not fared as well. As the reader can recall, the logic for this latter strategy is that opponents (negotiators), (1) because they hold to norms of equity (Adams, 1965), distributive justice (Homans, 1961), or reciprocity (Gouldner, 1960), (2) reciprocate the negotiators' (opponents') concessions, and (3) expect their own concessions to be reciprocated.

With regard to the first assumption, the studies by Adams, Gouldner, and Homans have demonstrated that individuals exhibit norms of equity and so forth in various encounters; to date, however, no one has demonstrated that these norms are brought to or felt to be relevant to the negotiation relationship. Since the negotiation relationship is distinct in several ways from other exchange relationships (Strauss, 1978), it seems reasonable to question whether or not these norms automatically would be extrapolated to negotiation. Also, such an extrapolation is open to question, because strong norms of competitiveness, achievement, and the need to maintain face in negotiations have evolved in many societies and might wash out any effects of the equity norm in negotiations. Likewise, in many arenas, the perception and label persist that a person's bargaining counterpart is an "opponent."

The first assumption has not been tested, but the latter two facets have. Tests of whether the opponent (negotiator) reciprocates the negotiator's (opponent's) concessions have not been supportive. If the assumption were valid, we would expect the opponent to follow a negotiator's large concession with a large concession and to follow a small concession with a small concession. Tests found this not to be the case (Wall, 1981a); rather than reciprocate the negotiators' concessions, opponents either repeated their prior concessions when they were followed by large negotiator concessions or altered their concessions when they were followed by small negotiator concessions.

Finally, we turn to the studies of the final assumption underpinning the reciprocity strategy—that negotiators (or opponents) expect their concessions to be reciprocated. Given the works of Adams (1965), Gouldner (1960), and Homans (1961), which show that people expect equity, reciprocity, and justice in their exchanges with others, it seems reasonable to expect that negotiators and opponents initially, when they have few indicators as to the other party's concession making, expect reciprocity from them. Specifically, when negotiators make a concession, they expect the opponent to reciprocate that concession. If the opponent fulfills this expectation, it also seems reasonable to posit that the negotiator again concedes and again expects the opponent to reciprocate.

What happens to the negotiator's reciprocity expectation when the opponent fails to reciprocate? Since negotiators change their expectations about the opponents' behavior as they note the opponents' responses to their concessions (Harsanyi, 1962), it appears that the opponents' failure to reciprocate would modify this expectation. Is the change shortlived or more permanent? This is an important question given the previously noted findings that opponents do not always reciprocate negotiator concessions.

Research undertaken to answer these questions and to test the assumption that negotiators initially expect reciprocity from opponents revealed that negotiators initially do expect reciprocity from the opponent (Wall, 1981a). However, once the expectation has been disconfirmed, they no longer expect reciprocity, and the expectation remains permanently altered.

Reinforcement Strategy

Like the reciprocity strategy, the reinforcement strategy modifies opponents' behavior through alterations of their NOs. Like both the LOA and reciprocity strategies, it works well at times and not so well at others. The strategy is labeled *reinforcement* because it is based on the principle that the opponent repeats behavior that is reinforced (Skinner, 1969). Inasmuch as opponents value the concessions made by negotiators, negotiators can use their own concessions as reinforcements for large (or acceptable) opponent concessions. Specifically, negotiators can give concessions (reinforcements) whenever opponents make acceptable concessions and thus increase the opponents' future concessions.

Practically speaking, the reinforcement strategy differs from the reciprocity strategy in only two ways. The first is that negotiators, when employing the reinforcement strategy, follow an acceptable opponent concession with their own large concession. They do not precede the opponent concession with a large concession, hoping that the opponent will reciprocate their generosity. Rather, negotiators wait and reinforce.

Second, the concessions negotiators employ in the reinforcement strategy do not match the opponents' concessions exactly; rather they exceed them by a small, conspicuous amount. The reason for the small increment is that in most cases opponents, after making a concession, feel they deserve the negotiator's matching concession; therefore, the matching concession is judged as "expected" reciprocity rather than as an appreciated reward or gesture. The conspicuous extra concession, in contrast, is viewed as a reward and a signal that the negotiator wishes to engage in future cooperative exchanges.

Although the logic underlying the reinforcement strategy is sound, the effects of the strategy have proved somewhat mixed. It has been found that opponents of a negotiator who uses a reward strategy concede more and agree more quickly than do opponents of a negotiator not using the strategy (Wall, 1977). Furthermore, the large opponent concessions continue even after the negotiator ceases to reward the opponent's concessions. However, the potency of the reinforcement strategy suffers whenever a constituent oversees the opponent's bargaining. The opponent, feeling accountable to the constituent (Klimoski, 1972; Klimoski & Ash, 1974), is less susceptible to external influence, does not respond to the negotiator's rewards, and thereby resists the negotiator's attempts to move and direct him or her.

Graduated Reduction in Tension (GRIT) Strategy

The GRIT strategy is a mixed strategy—one in which the negotiator's concession-making shifts over the course of the negotiation. As do the formerly discussed strategies, this strategy also suffers from contingent validity. It was proposed by Charles Osgood (1959, 1962) in the late 1950s and early 1960s as a method for reducing tensions between the Soviet Union and the United States. Osgood was alarmed by reciprocal exchanges of the two superpowers in their cold, but belligerent, contests. One side would take action that was intended or perceived to be threatening to the other side. In turn, the other side reciprocated with a belligerent act, and the counterpart again responded. A mutually amplifying process ensued, with both sides becoming more hostile, more threatening, less trusting, and less trustworthy. Such a process made it difficult for one side to institute a de-escalation, for even if it announced its desire and intention to reduce tensions or to take some cooperative step, the behavior was seen as highly suspect or was perceived as a competitive ploy.

To defuse this costly, dangerous cycle, Osgood suggested that one side should undertake a number of small unilateral, announced, conciliatory initiatives (concessions), but in so doing should not reduce its capability to retaliate against the opponent. Additionally, the initiating side should invite, but not demand, reciprocity from the opponent. His GRIT strategy, which encompasses these ideas, differs significantly from the LOA, reciprocity, and reinforcement strategies along a number of dimensions. It is more complex; it is designed for specific parties and circumstances; and it is not easily tested.

The last characteristic has presented some problems in establishing the validity of the strategy. However, the strategy can be tested somewhat by examining the validity of its facets or assumptions. Lindskold (1976), in a surgical examination of GRIT, has provided such an examination. He succinctly listed each of the detailed ten points of the Osgood strategy and then reviewed the existing literature to glean information on the validity of each.

Osgood's (1959, 1962) ten points are as follows:

1. The strategy must be designed and communicated in a manner that emphasizes the initiator's intent to reduce tension.
2. The initiator must publicly announce each initiative, indicating what it is, when it will take place, and where it will take place.
3. Each initiative must be carried out on schedule.
4. The opponent should be invited to reciprocate, but no demand for reciprocation should be made.
5. Initiatives must be continued over time, even in the absence of reciprocation.
6. Initiatives must be unambiguous and verifiable.
7. The initiatives should not impair the initiator's capability to retaliate against the opponent.
8. Likewise, the initiatives should not constrain the initiator from responding with graded responses to the opponent's escalations.
9. Initiatives should be diversified.
10. When reciprocation is obtained, the initiator should take subsequent steps that provide slightly less conciliation.

Lindskold finds support for Items 1, 2, 7, 8, and 10 and notes that Items 4, 5, and 9 are not supported. Item 3 drew mixed support. A review of the relevant studies revealed that imprecise and noncredible cooperative announcements definitely did not facilitate reciprocity, whereas credible initiatives did. However, these latter initiatives were more efficacious when the initiator possessed retaliation capability.

Item 6—conciliatory initiatives must be unambiguous and verifiable—also has mixed support. Hornstein and Deutsch (1967) found that the opportunity to inspect or verify the behavior of the opponent promoted the negotiator's trust of the opponent. Voluntary inspection, indeed, provides such trust; however, mandatory inspection probably leads to reduced trust. As Strickland (1958) and Kruglanski (1970) found, a subordinate who has worked without surveillance is considered more trustworthy than is one who has been monitored; analogously, it seems logical to surmise that less trust will be given to an inspected opponent than to one who is not inspected.

Summary

This chapter focused on the negotiation strategy, emphasizing that in the development of a strategy, the negotiator must choose goals, sort among the available tactics, and then weave the appropriate ones into an effective plan. It demonstrated the nuts and bolts of such a process, providing suggestions for the manner in which strategy development should unfold in complex, as well as simple, negotiations. The chapter then delineated several strategies that fold together various sets of tactics into coherent plans of action. The discussion closed with two observations: (1) negotiations and their settings are complex, and therefore considerable time and energy must be devoted to the development of a strategy that pursues the selected goals; and (2) a single strategy, either simple or complex, cannot be used in all situations, because, as our review demonstrated, the effectiveness of any strategy is situation contingent.

Two important threads of the preceding arguments focused on the situation (namely, the prescription calling for the elimination of tactics that do not support the negotiator's goals in the bargaining setting and the proposition that strategy effectiveness is situation contingent). Therefore, our attention now should turn to a more detailed evaluation of the situational elements in negotiation.

Chapter 6

Negotiation Situation

• In the development of a negotiation strategy, the pivotal underpinning is a set of decision rules or diagnostic questions generated by the negotiator to protect or serve as guides toward the targeted goals. Diagnostic questions include those like the following: (1) Does the negotiator's power exceed that of the opponent? If so, eliminate the reward tactics. (2) Do coercive tactics render the opponent independent of the negotiation? If so, eliminate the coercive tactics. Such questions were used to protect the goals of high NOs and an amicable future negotiator-opponent relationship. Each of these questions must be answered in order to sort the negotiation tactics.

To respond correctly to these queries and thereby to develop a valid strategy, negotiators must research the negotiation setting; in so doing, they must methodically comb through obvious as well as more obscure details in search of relevant information. What are the facets of the situation that are germane to the negotiation? That is, which answer the diagnostic queries? The following pages will respond to this question. Specifically, this chapter will present a detailed coverage of the situational factors and then focus on the rules protecting the negotiation goals.

The coverage of the situational factors will be detailed, and the reason for the thoroughness is twofold. First, no other source at present provides this information. Equally important, the scrutiny is proffered to provide a disciplined guide to negotiators for answering strategic questions. When exploring the environment, most negotiators use, or are victims of, perceptual economies. That is, they perceive what they expect to perceive; they see what they want to see; they form first impressions; they attend to the most salient, although not the most relevant, information; they attend to familiar stimuli; and they glean the most easily acquired data. To answer their strategic questions validly, negotiators must overcome these inclinations. It is hoped that the following pages can assist negotiators in doing so by delineating factors they often ignore.

Having delineated the facets of the negotiation situation, the chapter will explain the rules protecting the negotiator's goals. It will discuss the situational factors that provide answers to questions like these: What resources does the negotiator possess? Should the opponent's behavior be reinforced? Is dissatisfaction to the negotiator's benefit? And is the opponent's CL_{alt} high or low?

Overview

Upon initial consideration, the variety of possible negotiation situations seems unlimited and thereby unyielding to intelligible discussion. However, if we start at the core of the negotiation—considering the negotiation per se,—and then work our way out through the concentric circles housing the other elements of the situation (Exhibit 6–1), the discussion becomes more manageable.

Negotiation Per Se

The negotiation per se consists of the negotiation's nature, the issues, and the range of alternative outcomes (Exhibit 6–2). The negotiation's nature can be one-shot, repeated, sequential, serial, multiple, or linked (Strauss, 1978).

The most obvious facet of the issues in a negotiation is their number. The negotiation can cover one issue or a multitude of issues. Likewise, the issues can vary in importance; they can be as mundane as where a person eats or as important as the topics in the SALT negotiations.

In the same vein as the number and importance of the issues lies the complexity component. Issues can be very simple (for example, does the customer purchase the radio, or doesn't she?) or very complex (for example, does the hospital allow a seventeen-year-old girl to

Exhibit 6-1. Negotiation Situation.

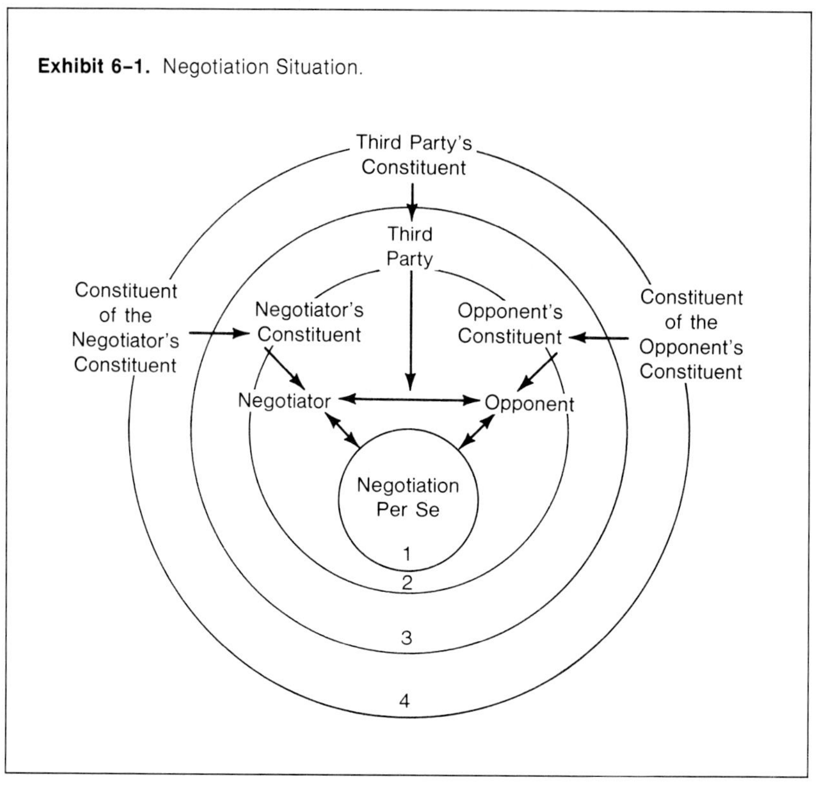

have an abortion without her parents' knowledge, or doesn't it?). The complexity is seldom independent of the number and importance facets in that an important issue has an uncanny way of becoming complex, and a complex issue, when closely scrutinized, generally reveals several subissues that make it up.

Prominence and tangibility are additional issue facets. Prominence can arise from a variety of sources. An issue can be visibly prominent, such as where a worker's office is located in relation to the boss's office. Likewise, an issue can be ethically prominent, as are the negotiations in the legal system, which bring some people to trial and punishment and allow others to go free. Finally, an issue can be culturally prominent; for instance, the Israeli government traded away thousands of square miles in the Camp David Accords, but just imagine the reaction of the Israeli nation if it had traded away the small strip of land under the Wailing Wall.

Tangible negotiation issues typically are those that can be

Exhibit 6–2. Negotiation Per Se.

Nature

- One-shot
- Repeated
- Sequential
- Serial
- Multiple
- Linked

Issues

- Number
- Importance
- Complexity
- Prominence
- Tangibility
- Sequencing
- Interdependence

Range of alternative outcomes

- Interdependence
- Number of feasible agreement points
- Number of alternatives
- Payoffs at each alternative
- Constraints

touched or perceived, and intangibles are those that cannot. The intangibles contain issues such as respect, love, goodwill, reputation, rights of entry, access, safety, esteem, danger, restraint, obligations, and allegiances, whereas the tangibles are more obvious—cows, houses, dogs, beer, cars, husbands, money, guns, fish, oil, and so on.

When more than one issue is under negotiation, the relationship between or among them generates two important issue facets: sequencing and interdependence. Sequencing is more quickly dealt with. Some items must be dealt with simultaneously; some, sequentially; and others, either way. It is probably obvious that interdependence represents one end of the continuum and independence, the other. Fortunately, many issues are independent, allowing the negotiator and opponent to resolve one and progress to the others. At the other end of the continuum lie the totally interdependent issues—those for which an agreement on one determines the level of agreement on another. For example, in many municipalities the wages of police and fire fighters are totally interdependent. If the city's representative negotiates a certain wage with the police force's representative, the fire fighters' wage is set at the same level.

Most issues lie at neither end of the continuum; rather, they are somewhat interdependent, and agreement or negotiation upon one alters the negotiation and agreement upon the others. In some cases, the interdependence is indigenous to the issues (for example, giving a person a promotion has an expected impact upon his or her salary). At other times, the interdependence is generated by the negotiating parties, as when President Carter "linked" U.S. grain negotiations with the Soviet Union to the Soviet behavior in Afghanistan. At still other times, outside events create interdependence among issues.

The discussion of the interdependence among the issues provides a convenient bridge to the next component of the negotiation per se: the range of alternative outcomes. The negotiator's and opponent's outcomes, like the issues, can vary in interdependence. They can be independent or totally interdependent. However, with this latter arrangement arises the question, What is the nature of the interdependence? There are two possible answers: integrative and distributive.

To present a better development of the concepts of integrative interdependence, distributive interdependence, and independence of outcomes, let us again borrow from the economists. On the left axes in Exhibit 6–3, the outcomes to the negotiator are represented by points on the vertical axis and the outcomes to the first opponent, by points on the horizontal axis. Assume that any of the alternative settlement points located within the axes and the curved line are attainable. Assume also that the negotiator and first opponent (perhaps two Mideastern neighbors negotiating over oil rights in a disputed area) are quickly closing toward an agreement on Alternative A (they divide the land fifty-fifty) when they recognize that other feasible agreement points exist, among them Alternatives B and C. In their subsequent debate, they realize that movement to Alternative B (the oil-rich nation takes 25 percent of the land, and the technologically advanced country contributes the expertise and equipment to develop the 25 percent) increases the negotiator's outcomes from N_1 to N_2 and increases the first opponent's outcomes from FO_1 to FO_2. If they continue the movement to Alternative C (the oil-rich nation takes 40 percent and throws in capital to help the technologically advanced country develop

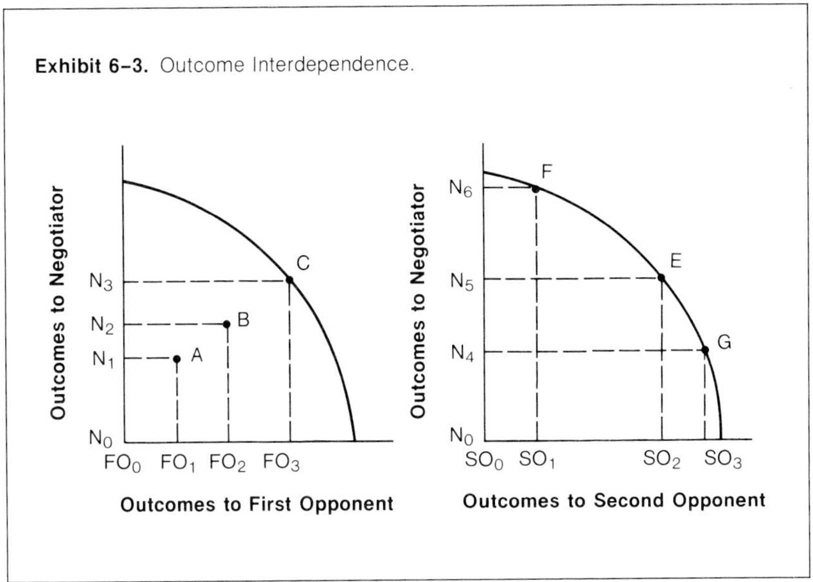

Exhibit 6–3. Outcome Interdependence.

the resources of both nations), the total gain to the negotiator is from N_1 to N_3 (or $N_3 - N_1$) and to the opponent, from FO_1 to FO_3 (or $FO_3 - FO_1$).

Thus, this represents integrative interdependence. Alternatives A, B, and C are the options open to the negotiator and first opponent, and by moving out from the N_0FO_0 origin, each party increases its outcomes as the other increases its own.

In contrast, the situation could be like the one represented by the right axes, where only Alternatives E, F, and G are viable options (the negotiator's oil loss is the opponent's gain and vice versa). In this case, the negotiator's and opponent's outcomes would be distributively interdependent. An improvement for the negotiator (say, from E to F, which yields an increase of $N_6 - N_5$) results in degeneration of the second opponent's outcomes (from SO_2 to SO_1, or a loss of $SO_2 - SO_1$). Likewise, an improvement for the second opponent (say, from E to G, an outcome increase of $SO_3 - SO_2$) generates a setback for the negotiator from N_5 to N_4, or a loss of $N_5 - N_4$.

As Exhibit 6–3 depicts, the outcomes of the first and second opponents are independent (perhaps one is the negotiator's northern neighbor and the other, the negotiator's southern neighbor). That is, a change in one's outcomes (for example, from FO_2 to FO_3 for the first opponent) has no effect on those of the other.

Exhibit 6–3, with some minor modifications, assists us in discussing the other facets within the range of alternative outcomes category in Exhibit 6–2. One facet is the number of positions or alternatives at which the negotiator and opponent can agree (Joseph & Wilks, 1963); for instance, the negotiator and first opponent in Exhibit 6–3 might have had twelve, as opposed to three, points at which they could settle.

Somewhat akin to the number of positions of possible agreement is the constraint facet. As depicted in Exhibit 6–4, negotiators and opponents might have constraints limiting their options. Note that, of the options (A, B, C, D, E, F, G, and H), only one, C, lies outside the feasible set established by Constraint 1. If Constraints 2 and 3 were added, the negotiating parties would find only Points A and B as viable options.

Moving out from the core negotiation, its nature, the issues, and the range of alternative outcomes, we encounter the primary actors in the negotiation: the negotiator, the opponent, and the relationship between them.

Negotiator's (or Opponent's) Characteristics, Goals, and Experience

Characteristics

The negotiator and opponent as individuals possess a wide possible variety in situational dimensions (Exhibit 6–5). Each negotiator can be classified according to physiological characteristics, such as height, weight, sex, age, and race. Consideration of the personal or psychological factors brings to mind each negotiator's intelligence, personality, motivations, perceptual biases, attitudes, and bargaining orientations. Group or social factors include nationality, religion, social status, culture, and so on. And salient behavioral differences are noted in such characteristics as dress, speech, aggressiveness, inquisitiveness, competitiveness, and altruism.

Goals

As important but less salient than the negotiator's and opponent's characteristics are their goals and prior experience. Goals (or CL), as noted earlier, can be from high to low. Likewise, they can be hostile or conciliatory (Crow & Noel, 1965); individualistic, competitive, or altruistic; and aligned with norms of equality or equity.

Exhibit 6–4. Negotiation Constraints.

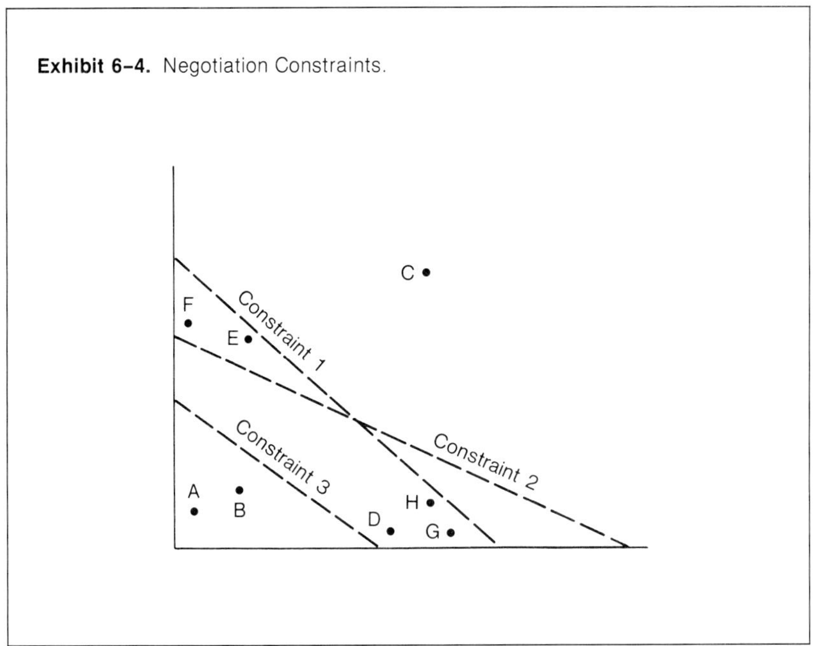

Experience

The most obvious aspect of the parties' past experience is the presence or absence of negotiation exposure (Conrath, 1970), which can lie along a possibly lengthy continuum; a negotiator may have engaged in only one negotiation or survived thousands. He or she might have been a negotiator for twenty minutes or fifty years. Given that the negotiator or opponent has negotiation experience, the type of experience then assumes some importance. The experience could have been of a hostile versus friendly nature (McClintock & McNeel, 1967) or rewarding as opposed to unrewarding (Harrison & McClintock, 1965).

Negotiator-Opponent Relationship

Whereas the negotiator's and opponent's characteristics, goals, and prior experience contribute many of the situational factors in the second orb, others are proffered by the relationship between them, a relationship that can be cleaved neatly into two components: process and structure (Exhibit 6–6).

Exhibit 6–5. Negotiator's (or Opponent's) Characteristics, Goals, and Experience.

Characteristics

- Physiological
  - Height
  - Weight
  - Sex
  - Age
  - Race
- Personal or psychological
  - Intelligence
  - Personality
  - Motivations
  - Perceptual biases
  - Attitudes
  - Bargaining orientations
- Group or social
  - Nationality
  - Religion
  - Social status
  - Culture
- Behavioral
  - Dress
  - Speech
  - Aggressiveness
  - Inquisitiveness
  - Competitiveness
  - Altruism

Goals

- Level
- Hostility level
- Individualistic, competitive, or altruistic nature
- Equality or equity alignment

Experience

- Exposure level
- Number of prior negotiations
- Time as negotiator
- Nature of previous encounters

The processes unfolding in the negotiator-opponent relationship—the different maneuvers, tactics, strategies, communications, and other exchange behaviors of the parties—have been discussed previously. An additional facet of the process involves the location and differences in the negotiator's and opponent's initial positions (Johnson, 1967).

Exhibit 6–6. Negotiator-Opponent Relationship.

Process

Initial positions
Maneuvers
Tactics
Strategies
Negotiation phase
Hostility and cooperation/conflict phase
Trust
Perceptions of each other
Attributions to each other
Payoffs to each

Structure

Number of negotiation roles
Number of parties per role
Symmetry of role occupancies
Communication structure
Power
Status

They may be compatible in that the parties' CL or limits overlap or are somewhat closely aligned, or they may be incompatible in that the positions, aspirations, or limits are quite far apart.

In addition to the initial positions and interparty maneuvers, tactics, strategies, and so forth, the phases in negotiation can differ significantly. Earlier we discussed the negotiation steps per se: (1) establishment of the negotiation range; (2) reconnaissance of the negotiation range; and (3) closure. The negotiation flows through these negotiation phases and concomitantly through hostility phases. Like a sine curve, the negotiation can go up and down; it can continually wind down; or it can snowball.

The initial facet of the structural aspect in the negotiator-opponent relationship is the number of negotiation roles. To this point the discussion has assumed there were two roles—the negotiator and opponent—but this is not a sacred number. As United Nations conferences, NATO meetings, congressional hearings, staff meetings, and family discussions reveal, the number of negotiator roles can become quite large. Within each role the number of negotiators also can vary. The obvious lower limit is one per role, and theoretically there is no upper limit in number; however, as a practical matter, a negotiation team seldom is composed of more than ten people.

Another structural facet surfaces with the number of negotiators per role: the symmetry of the role occupancies. The roles can be occupied quite symmetrically, as would be the case when five labor negotiators sit down with five management negotiators. The occupancy also can be quite asymmetric, as when a U.S. businessman sits down to parley with a Chinese trade delegation.

The communication structure between or among the negotiators and opponents typically is assumed to be face to face. However, many negotiations (and an increasing number) are not face to face; they are conducted over the telephone or via letter (Gest, 1981). Thus, communications can be verbal, written, face to face, distant, one way, or two way. Finally, the negotiator and opponent may choose to communicate through intermediaries rather than directly.

In addition to these structural elements, the relationship between the negotiator and opponent also can be classified in terms of status and power relationships. For each of these factors, it is best to think of the relationship in absolute, as well as relative, terms. Note that both the negotiator and opponent can be of high status, as was the case when Egyptian President Anwar as-Sadat and Israeli Prime Minister Menachem Begin met at Camp David. Both can be of low status, as were the parties negotiating and hammering out the translation details of the U.S.–North Vietnam settlement. One party can have high status and the other, low, such as when a captain's wife negotiates tacitly with the general's wife over territory at a cocktail party.

Remember that the negotiator's status and power seldom are determined solely within his interaction with the opponent. Rather, status and power result in part from the negotiator's alternatives, his relationships with third parties, and the group from which he hails—his constituency.

Negotiator-Constituent Relationship

As Exhibit 6–7 shows, the negotiator's relationships with his constituents (and the opponent's relationship with his own constituents) are quite analogous to his relationship with the opponent, for the negotiator finds himself negotiating with, as well as representing, the constituency. Like the relationship with an opponent, a relationship with a constituent can be viewed in terms of its structure and process. Consider the structure first. The most obvious dimension is whether or not

Exhibit 6–7. Negotiator (Opponent)–Constituent Relationship.

Structure

- Existence of constituent
- Negotiator's role
- Negotiator's membership
- Constituent's and negotiator's status
- Constituent's and negotiator's power
- Number of constituents
- Cohension of constituency
- Centralization of constituency structure

Process

- Negotiator's maneuvers
- Negotiator's tactics
- Negotiator's strategies
- Constituent's monitoring
- Constituent's evaluations
- Constituent's feedback
- Constituent's trust
- Constituent's rewards
- Constituent's punishments
- Constituent's threats

the negotiator has a constituent. The second question deals with the negotiator's role. Is the negotiator allowed any discretion, or is he or she merely a mail carrier who delivers the constituent's negotiation messages? A similar structural element concerns whether or not the negotiator is a group member or a free-lance representative. A manager negotiating with a superior provides an example of the former case, and a lawyer representing a college basketball player in a contract negotiation with a National Basketball Association (NBA) team is an example of the latter.

If the negotiator is a constituency member, several other structural dimensions assume primary importance. Paramount among these are the status and power of the negotiator and constituents. As was true within the negotiator-opponent relationship, these factors should be considered here absolutely, as well as relatively, because four combinations are possible. For example, the negotiator and opponent both can have low power (or status), or both can have high power (or status). The negotiator can have high power (or status) absolutely but not relatively (for example, as Dobrynin had as a Soviet negotiator). In contrast, like a king who is negotiating on the behalf of a small kingdom group, a negotiator can have weak absolute, but strong relative, power (or status).

The structural elements within the constituency include the number of constituents, the cohesion of the constituency, and the centralization of its structure.

The process elements include the negotiator's maneuvers, tactics, strategies, and other actions or reactions toward the constituent. However, the factors that appear to be most relevant in observed negotiations are those emanating from the constituency. In most cases, the negotiator represents or is responsible to a superior of higher status and power. Therefore, the constituents' monitoring, evaluations, feedback, trust (or lack thereof), rewards, punishments, and threats are potent in their alterations of the negotiator's behavior and the negotiation process.

Interconstituent Factors

The relationship between the two constituencies, like the constituent-negotiator relationship, can be depicted along structural and process lines (Exhibit 6–8). Two sets of factors appear most important for the structural dimension. The first entails the strengths of the two constituencies, with correlates no doubt including size, status, resources, and power bases of each constituency. This strength again must be viewed from both the absolute and relative perspective, yet the relative strength seems more important to the negotiation. Constituencies of approximately equal strength seldom attempt to influence or alter the others' behavior; rather, such attempts more often occur where there is strength asymmetry.

The second major structural facet of the interconstituent relationship is the communication channel. Does one exist? This aspect often is overlooked; we assume that channels between constituencies do exist, because we feel constituencies can just talk to each other. For several reasons, few of these "backchannels" are operational: (1) communication responsibility usually is delegated to the negotiators; (2) the constituents are oriented mainly toward intragroup, as opposed to intergroup, communication; (3) the establishment of interconstituent channels requires time and money, and therefore, inertia works against them; and (4) there appears to be a norm against interconstituent communication. It is the rare problem—the big exception (for example, the

Exhibit 6–8. Interconstituent and Third-Party Factors.

Interconstituent Factors

- Structure
  - Constituencies' strengths
  - Size of constituencies
  - Constituencies' status
  - Constituencies' resources and power bases
  - Communication channels
- Process
  - Existence and frequency of communication
  - Nature of communiqués
  - Constituents' maneuvers
  - Constituents' tactics
  - Constituents' strategies

Third-Party Factors

- Structure
  - Presence (actual and potential)
  - Role
  - Number of persons per role
  - Power
  - Status
- Process
  - Influence upon negotiator-opponent relationship
  - Influence upon negotiator (opponent)
  - Influence upon negotiator-constituency relationship
  - Influence upon constituents
  - Influence upon interconstituent relationship
  - Influence upon environment–negotiation system relationship

R. J. Reynolds–Rothman's merger)—that is to be discussed by the constituents. Opposing constituents who wish to open channels, therefore, are judged out of line.

The use of the communication channel brings us to the process side of the interconstituent relationship. The first consideration is whether or not the existing channel is used. If it is, the frequency of communication is relevant, as is the nature of the communiqués. Once communication and subsequent interaction with the counterpart have been undertaken by the constituents, their exchange can assume all the characteristics of the interaction taking place between the negotiator and the opponent. Specifically, each can maneuver, undertake tactical ploys, implement strategies, threaten, or undertake any combination of behaviors.

Third-Party Factors

Third parties typically are thought of as persons making inputs into the negotiation in order to enhance the harmony of the exchange and the probability of agreement. Their presence and the behaviors they undertake contribute significantly to the situational variety of the negotiation.

From a structural perspective, the first consideration is whether or not there is a third party present at the negotiation; the second is whether or not one potentially could enter the process (Pruitt & Johnson, 1970). The role of the third party next assumes importance; this party can serve as an intermediary, mediator, fact finder, or arbitrator or can combine any number of the roles. The third party can serve alone, with a colleague, or as a member of a large bevy. Finally, the third party's power and status in relation to the constituents have an extensive possible range. In general, intermediaries have no power; mediators, low power; fact finders, moderate power; and arbitrators, high power. All the roles, with the exception of the intermediary, usually are of high status.

From the procedural angle, the third party's behavior toward the other parties and theirs toward the third party are dictated somewhat by role. (Looking at the extremes, the intermediary typically is little more than a mail carrier, whereas the arbitrator, acting as sort of judge, ends the negotiation with a ruling.) However, regardless of role, any third party can affect the negotiation by influencing and interacting with six leverage points: (1) the negotiator-opponent relationship; (2) the negotiator (and opponent); (3) the negotiator-constituency relationship; (4) the constituents; (5) the interconstituent relationship; and (6) the environment–negotiation system relationship (Wall, 1981b).

Environmental Factors

The final sector of situational variables springs from the environment—the persons, groups, and institutions with whom the negotiation is interdependent. This negotiation-environment dependency has two principal antecedents: (1) parties to the negotiation have ties to persons, groups, and institutions in the environment, and (2) the negotiation, along with the exchanges within it, has implicit and explicit consequences for parties in the environment. Given their interdependency with the negotiation, many "outsiders" take steps to alter the negotiation, and their actions produce many of the situational variants for the negotiation. In addition, many environmental factors and parties inadvertently alter the negotiation.

The environmental factors in a negotiation are shown in Exhibit 6–9. Time pressure generally arises external to the negotiation. (For example, a manager may tell two subordinates to resolve their differences by noon or face the manager's intervention. A natural time limit exists for farm workers and farm owners who negotiate as the fruit ripens.) This time pressure may be mild or acute (Pruitt & Drews, 1969) and in the form of deadlines (Bass, 1966) or costs for time (Komorita & Barnes, 1969). Both seem to reduce the parties' CL and demands. As Stevens (1963) notes,

> An approaching deadline puts pressure on the parties to state their true positions and thus does much to squeeze elements of bluff out of the later stages of negotiation. However, an approaching deadline does much more. . . . It brings pressures to bear which actually change the least favorable terms upon which each party is willing to settle. Thus it operates as a force tending to bring about conditions necessary for agreement. (p. 100)

Cultural norms represent a second set of environmental influences. As Harnett and Cummings (1980) and other authors note, different nationalities bargain differently. Some start high, whereas others open with their final offer. The author was quite amused by the initial frustration of a Turkish friend who was attempting to purchase a house in a midwestern town. All the houses, it seemed, were overpriced. When asked how he bargained over the prices, the Turk, with a puzzled look in his eye, said he did not; as was his custom, he looked at the house, commenting quite favorably upon what he saw, and then asked for the price. If it was too high, he simply said so politely and left, never to return with a lower counteroffer.

Some cultures dictate that negotiators be abusive; others demand conciliatory behavior. Some reinforce specificity; others, vagueness. The list of cultural differences could continue, revealing some striking variants, but none more pronounced than the one once noted in the negotiation between two Quaker farmers over the price for some bovine destruction. The first Friend's cow had broken through his fence and enjoyed several hearty meals in the second's corn fields. Thus, the stage was set for a negotiation over the proper remuneration. The cow's owner, after walking through the corn, surmised that the damage was \$100. The corn owner's reply was that the damage was \$20.

Exhibit 6–9. Environmental Factors.

Time pressure

Cultural norms

Precedents

Support for negotiator or opponent

Visibility of negotiation

Constituents of constituents

- Existence
- Structural and procedural factors

Third parties' constituents

- Existence
- Structural and procedural factors

Interdependency of negotiation and environment

- Dependence of environment upon negotiation
- Dependence of negotiation upon environment
- Environment's power
- Environment's size
- Environment's munificence
- Environment's stability

In the next round of this less-than-belligerent negotiation, the cow owner conceded $20, stating that he could go no lower, because he was certain that the destroyed area would have produced $80 of corn at harvest. The corn owner conceded only $10, stating that he could accept no more than $30, because he had only that amount invested in the destroyed area (in seeds, fertilizer, gasoline, and labor). To make an odd negotiation even odder, the Friends deadlocked—$50 apart. After a few minutes, the cow owner dredged up a compromise. The corn owner, after selling his harvested corn crop, would estimate the value of the lost corn, and the cow owner would pay it without question. However, the corn owner had to promise beforehand that the price would be "fair" to himself. There should be no question in the reader's mind as to the price quoted in the autumn.

Just as culture does, precedents within the nonlegal, as well as the legal, arenas impinge upon the outcomes and process of negotiations (Schelling, 1960). Not as intuitively clear as the previously discussed effects, but probably just as potent, is the environmental support for either the negotiator or opponent. As Lall (1966) notes, the 1960s saw a significant support for the less developed countries in their negotiations with the developed countries. Over the years there have been shifts in popular support for unions in their negotiation with management. Support for women in all endeavors, including negotiations, increased during the 1970s.

In addition to supporting specific groups, the environment also can foster and reward certain types of negotiation behavior. At present, the legal environment in several states—especially California—rewards attorney behavior that results in settlements as opposed to rewarding behavior that takes disputes to court. In Missouri, however, the legal environment is not as supportive of this behavior.

The effects of culture, precedent, and reward structures are enhanced by the visibility of the negotiation. If a negotiation is not open, the lack of visibility serves as a buffer to the system, whereas if it is open, the parties feel the full impact of the environment.

Situational variety also is contributed by the constituents of the constituents and the constituents of the third parties. For both sets of "second-order" constituents, the question surfaces as to whether or not they exist; if they do, they contribute structural and procedural variety to the bargaining situation. Consider the constituents' constituents; their number, role, cohesion, structure, power, and status may vary considerably, and their behavioral exchange with the constituents can vary along the lines of maneuvers, tactics, rewards, punishments, and so on.

Similarly, the third parties' constituents foster situational factors. As do the constituents of the negotiators and constituents, they contribute structural and procedural variety to the bargaining situation. This variety and its influence are worth noting, because scholars seemingly have ignored the third parties' relationship to their constituency. This is unfortunate, because the third parties' constituents, if they do exist, are not disinterested parties. Rather, they most often hold the third parties responsible for an agreement. For example, the Federal Mediation and Conciliation Service reviews the proficiency of its mediators in obtaining agreements. President Reagan in May 1981 closely monitored Special Envoy Philip Habib's attempts to strike an accord between Israel and Syria. Superiors typically evaluate their subordinates' capability to mediate the relationship among their own subordinates.

Recall from the earlier pages that the negotiation and environment can be highly interdependent. The environment can be highly dependent upon the process and outcome of a negotiation, as the United States was very dependent upon the steel negotiations during the 1950s (Cancio, 1959). In contrast, as in the negotiation between a doctor and a hospital administrator over the scheduling of the operating room, the environment can be independent of the negotiation.

The opposite side is the dependency of the negotiation upon the environment. The negotiation can be highly dependent upon elements in the environment, as would be any negotiation between the PLO and Israel in which the PLO would find itself heavily dependent upon the Arab states, and Israel would be dependent upon the United States.

Other factors to be considered in the interdependency between the negotiation and environment are the power of the environment, the size of the environment (that is, the number of people affected by and capable of affecting the negotiation), its munificence, and its stability.

Situational Factors as Guides to Strategy Development

As noted in the introduction to this chapter, the rationale for delineating the situational factors in a negotiation is twofold: first, the delineation from a theoretical perspective provides a thorough overview of the factors that affect the negotiation; it is these factors that dictate the effectiveness of the negotiation strategies. Second, the listings can guide negotiators in strategy development. They generate questions (for example, Is the negotiator's power greater than that of the opponent?) and seek answers that in turn determine the tactics they will employ. As we will now see, the previously delineated situational context provides the answers to these questions.

Simple Negotiations

Consider first the questions in strategy development for a simple negotiation (p. 78); for instance, Will the opponent be contingently effective? (that is, Will the opponent be cooperative if the negotiator cooperates?). The negotiator can attempt to glean an answer by first cooperating and then monitoring the opponent's responses. However, this approach has some built-in risks, which can be avoided by analyzing the situation.

By working their way through Exhibits 6–2 and 6–5 to 6–9, negotiators may note many facets that seem irrelevant to the question and then come to the interdependence of the NOs. In Exhibit 6–2, the negotiation situation provides a cue to the answer: if the opponents' NOs are distributively interdependent with those of the negotiators—what the negotiators gain, the opponents lose—the negotiators cannot expect contingent cooperation. The opponents probably will bargain competitively. In Exhibit 6–5, negotiators can consider the goals of the opponents (Are they competitive or altruistic?) and the nature of their previous encounters (Were they hostile or accommodating?). Continuing in Exhibit 6–5, the negotiation phase might be considered: in the first phase of the negotiation, opponents most often are noncooperative. Likewise, if the opponents have constituents—especially ones that monitor them closely or do not trust them—cooperation is not to be expected. And if the opponents' constituencies order them to be tough (Exhibit 6–7), the opponents will be competitive, regardless of the negotiators' behavior.

Turning to a second question suggested for a simple negotiation—Does the opponent have limited alternatives (CL_{alt})?—we must recall that the CL_{alt} is a set of alternatives to agreement that is composed of NOs from potential agreements with other parties, as well as the NOs from a simple nonagreement. Which situational facets provide information to the negotiator about the opponent's CL_{alt}? The first information comes from the range of alternative outcomes (Exhibit 6–2); the negotiator can estimate the number of alternatives open to the opponent (including nonagreement) and the probable costs and payoffs of the best alternative. Perhaps the plaintiff's attorney–defendant's attorney negotiation during a civil settlement best illustrates such a situation. The defendant's attorney can view the negotiation from the opposing attorney's point of view and surmise that the plaintiff's attorney has two alternatives to agreement at the current offer: withdrawing from the negotiation (that is, nonagreement, or dropping the case) or taking it to trial. The CL_{alt} of the former alternative is low and certain (no contingency fee plus the scorn of the client). As for the latter option, going to trial proffers high payoffs (for example, a 50 percent chance of the award) and high costs (for example, time in investigations, trial time, and frequent interactions with the client). The probability for the payoffs is moderate and that for the costs, certain. To estimate the plaintiff attorney's CL_{alt}, the defendant's attorney subjectively calculates the payoff for each of the two alternatives (for example, an amount less than $0 for dropping the case and $1,000 for going to trial). Given these calculations, the negotiator would conclude that the opponent has a very low CL_{alt}.

In considering the opponent's CL_{alt}, the negotiator also predicts the reactions of the opponent's constituent (if one exists) and other third parties to a deadlock or choice of alternatives to agreement (Exhibits 6–7 and 6–8). For instance, a termination or deadlock might portray the opponent as a hero in the constituent's eyes or engender constituency hostility. Likewise, the opponent's exercise of an alternative (for example, employing scabs to run the presses or purchasing foreign, as opposed to domestic, steel) could raise the ire of important third parties.

Finally, the negotiator needs to consider environmental factors in determining the opponent's probable CL_{alt} (Exhibit 6–9). Some cultural norms (for example, those of the Irish) and precedents (for example, those of the United Mine Workers) reward nonagreement, whereas others (for example, those of the Japanese and the steel workers, respectively) do not. In addition, perhaps the interdependence of the negotiation and environment is of utmost importance. If high interdependence exists and the environmental factors are powerful, the effect on the opponent's CL_{alt} can be awesome. Consider, for example, the factors being weighed by the Polish negotiators facing Lech Walesa in the early and middle months of 1981. These negotiators knew that the Soviet Union was closely watching Walesa's negotiation and that to the Kremlin, the control of its satellites and the cohesion of the Warsaw Pact countries were highly intertwined with the Polish negotiations. Thus, although the Soviets wanted an agreement with provisions acceptable to them, above all they wanted any agreement, because they viewed the ongoing negotiation, laced with its threats and innuendos, as highly destabilizing. The Soviets wanted closure and expressed a willingness to intervene if the agreement were not reached. Such pressures upon Walesa (the opponent), the Polish negotiators knew, eroded his CL_{alt} considerably.

Complex Negotiations

Having examined two questions used to guide the negotiator's strategy development for the simple negotiation, let us turn to the questions raised in the complex negotiation (p. 79). In the interest of time and space we focus upon two only: (1) Is the future negotiation/relationship with the opponent important? (2) Is the negotiator's power greater than that of the opponent? Consider the guidance provided by the situational factors.

The Future • Turning first to the question of whether the future negotiation/relationship is important, a perusal of the situational factors supplies substantial guidance. Of the factors of the negotiation per se (Exhibit 6–2), one of the most relevant is the nature of the negotiation. A one-shot negotiation generates a future relationship of less import than do repeated, sequential, or serial negotiations. In the latter three types, the future negotiations (especially if more than one) quite feasibly assume more importance than the present one. Multiple and linked negotiations also raise the value of future relationships, because, although possible, it is quite seldom that such negotiations can be conducted simultaneously.

Moving to the issues under negotiation discussed in Exhibit 6–2, a negotiator should consider the importance of any future negotiations. If they are of minor consequence, the negotiator can discount the future relationship. Correlated highly with the nature of the negotiation is the interdependence of the issues and outcomes under negotiation. If the issues (or outcomes) are highly interdependent, the negotiation is likely to be manifold; therefore, the future relationship appreciates in importance.

Exhibit 6–5 contains factors that have relevance—perhaps surprisingly so—for the question at hand. The sex, age, race, and nationality of the opponent has a fallout effect. Specifically, the negotiator at times finds that the maintenance of an amicable relationship and somewhat productive future negotiations with the current opponent is quite necessary—not for the outcomes of their relationship, but for the outcomes arising from negotiations with other opponents of the same sex, age, race, or nationality. For example, the United States wishes to retain an acceptable relationship and negotiation posture with the PLO, not because the positive interactions will bring benefits from the PLO. Instead, the harmony is expected to provide positive valences and more oil from the Arab countries.

When considering the opponent's goals (Exhibit 6–5), the negotiator uncovers another factor dictating the importance of the future negotiation and relationship. If the goals of the opponent—detected from self-reports or other investigative activity—are altruistic, cooperative, or integrative, continued negotiation and interaction with the opponent would seem to be to the negotiator's advantage. In contrast, if the goals are individualistic or competitive, the favorableness of future relationships must be discounted.

Look now at the structure of the negotiator-opponent relationship in Exhibit 6–6. If the opponent is but one of several negotiators on the opposing team, a strong relationship/negotiation is not highly advantageous; the opponent may be here today and gone tomorrow. In contrast, if the opponent is the leader or a powerful person on that team, the verdict should be quite different.

The negotiator-constituent relationship contains facets that provide answers to our question (Exhibit 6–7). If the negotiator finds that he or she has a constituent who perceives the future negotiation and relationship with the opponent to be important, then they are important to the negotiator. Such importance increases as the constituent overtly or tacitly spells out the importance of the future and uses threats, power, and status to ensure that the negotiator preserve and cultivate the future negotiation/relationship. Such a situation might not be immediately salient to the reader, even though such occurrences are omnipresent—a supervisor tells a salesperson that the customer *will* be satisfied; a political boss informs liaison offices that the future cooperation of a splinter coalition is essential; or a wife dictates to her husband that he ease up on a socially prominent opponent.

Coming to the interconstituent and third-party factors in Exhibit 6–8, the negotiator finds several that shed light on the query. One is that the negotiator-opponent relationship should parallel that between their constituents. If a harmonious state of affairs exists between the constituencies—as it does between the United States and Great Britain—the negotiator-opponent affair likewise should be free of discord. If the third parties or the institutions they represent deem the future negotiations and relationships to be of prime importance, the negotiator in many cases also may have to consider them of such a nature, especially when third parties are powerful enough to ensure that they get whatever they want.

Finally, looking at the environmental factors (Exhibit 6–9), we note that interdependence of the negotiation and environment generates pressure to keep the future negotiation and relationship on an even keel. Usually the environment is more powerful than the negotiator; therefore, if it depends on a continuously harmonious negotiator-opponent accord, it will bring strong pressure upon the negotiator to keep it harmonious. From the negotiator's perspective, the future negotiation/relationship becomes important because the environmental forces dictate that it is important and reward the negotiator for considering it so. Note, for example, how this all unfolds in the airline industry. Since for many years the sales of jet airplanes and engines in foreign markets have generated more foreign exchange than any other manufactured U.S. export, the U.S. economy is very dependent on harmonious negotiations/relationships between the airline manufacturers and the firms supplying their engines. If these negotiations were to sour—which they seldom do—the U.S. government would place strong pressure on the offending negotiators. In short, the negotiators from Boeing and General Electric have to consider that their future relationship is important, because strong forces—among them the U.S. government—say they are important.

Negotiator's Relative Power • The preceding pages demonstrate the manner in which an investigation of the situation allows a negotiator to determine whether or not the future relationship and negotiation with the opponent are important. Using Tables Exhibits 6–2 and 6–5 through 6–9 as guides, we now seek evidence as to whether or not the negotiator's power is greater than that of the opponent. The following is a list of the factors that would be relevant to the negotiator surveying the negotiation situation:

1. If the issues are more important to the opponent than to the negotiator, the negotiator has a power advantage (Exhibit 6–2).
2. If the opponent has more constraints than does the negotiator, the negotiator has more power (Exhibit 6–2).
3. When the negotiator is of an age, sex, race, or culture that is supported by the environment, the negotiator has a power advantage (Exhibit 6–5).
4. Superior intelligence and stronger aggressiveness on the negotiator's part provide a power advantage (Exhibit 6–5).
5. The negotiator with more bargaining experience than the opponent—number of negotiations and time as a negotiator—has a power advantage (Exhibit 6–5).
6. The negotiator with a larger bargaining team has a power advantage (Exhibit 6–6).
7. When the negotiator, as opposed to the opponent, has no constituency, the negotiator has more power (Exhibit 6–7).
8. If the opponent's constituency is not unified, the negotiator possesses a power advantage (Exhibit 6–7).
9. When the opponent's constituency monitors him or her closely and makes a thorough evaluation, the negotiator obtains a power advantage (Exhibit 6–7).

10. If the strength and size of the negotiator's constituency is greater than that of the opponent, the negotiator enjoys a power edge (Exhibit 6–8).
11. If the negotiator's constituents' maneuvers, tactics, and strategies are well designed and implemented, they give the negotiator a power edge over the opponent (Exhibit 6–8).
12. When the negotiator has power over an influential third party, it provides power over the opponent (Exhibit 6–8).
13. If the opponent is under more time pressure than is the negotiator, it is to the negotiator's power advantage (Exhibit 6–9).
14. When precedents are to the negotiator's advantage, the negotiator has more power (Exhibit 6–9).
15. If there is more environmental support for the negotiator than the opponent, the negotiator reaps more power (Exhibit 6–9).
16. Whenever the negotiator is less dependent on the environment than is the opponent, the negotiator has a power advantage (Exhibit 6–9).

This discussion and list guide the negotiator in answering two questions essential to the development of strategies for simple and complex negotiations. By using Exhibits 6–2 and 6–5 through 6–9 and by examining the situation in which the negotiation unfolds, the negotiator in a similar fashion can answer the other questions generated to protect the negotiation goals, close upon the appropriate negotiation tactics, and develop a contingently effective negotiation strategy.

Summary

Exhibit 6–10 serves as a recapitulation of the strategic development process. Initially, negotiators set the goals they wish to pursue in the negotiation (for example, high NOs). To ensure that these goals are served or protected, they develop a set of diagnostic questions or rules that will eliminate inappropriate tactics. These questions (for example, Is the negotiator more powerful than the opponent?) are answered by determining which facets of the negotiation are relevant to each question (for example, if the opponent is under more time pressure than is the negotiator, the negotiator has a power advantage). Using the answers (for example, the negotiator is more powerful) supplied by their investigation of the situation, negotiators eliminate some tactics (for example, reward tactics) and mesh the remainder into a strategy.

Exhibit 6–10. Development of a Negotiation Strategy.

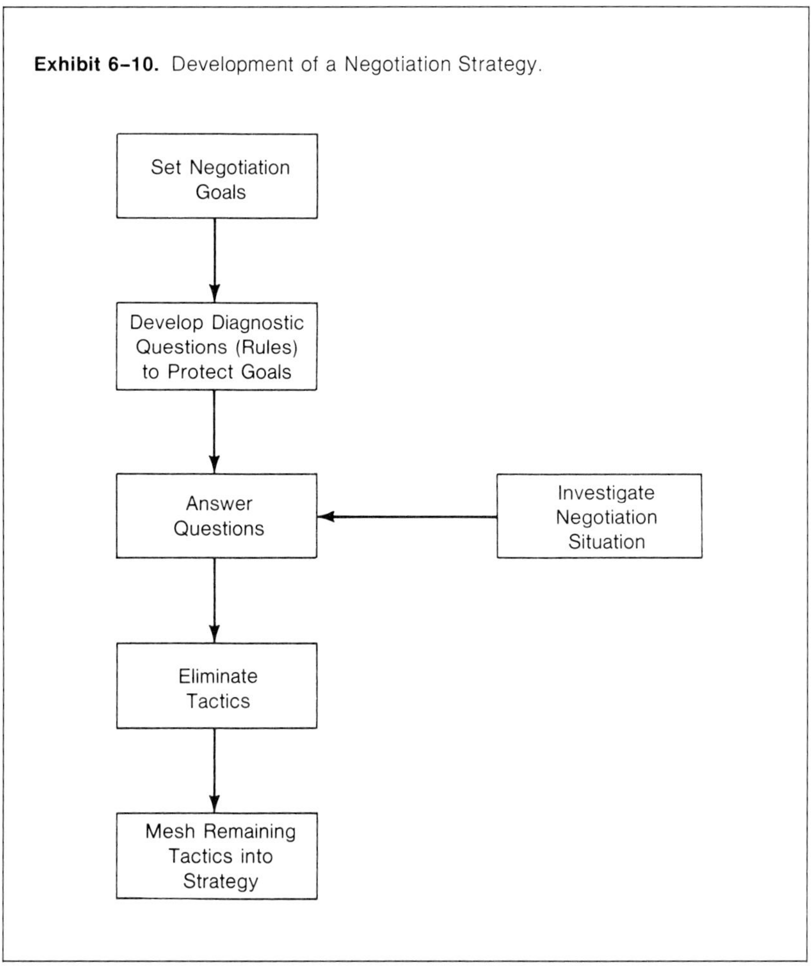

Chapter 7

Negotiations Applied

● Exhibit 7–1 illustrates the assertion made at the beginning of Chapter 1—negotiation is useful—and it is hoped that the cases and examples accompanying its logical development to this point have corroborated that pronouncement. Given this spadework, we now turn to a specific discussion of the levels at which negotiation is used—that is, the situations in which the information conveyed in the previous chapters is of use. First, we will look at the benefits and costs of negotiation in general and then discuss the applicability of negotiations to specific settings.

Benefits and Costs of Negotiations

In general, negotiation serves as a useful method for persons or groups to coordinate their behaviors, and it proves to be of signal importance because it can be used when other methods are not viable. For instance, the natives in Chapter 1's opening episode negotiated with the sailors even when other methods of coordination and communication were unavailable. Two army captains find negotiation useful because it fills the gap created by rank equality. Likewise, two surgeons or a surgeon and a pathologist find it a nice fallback whenever the friendly art of persuasion fails.

Negotiation need not substitute for other interpersonal and intergroup processes; in fact, it most frequently complements, greases, or aids those currently used. For example, I can require my secretary to type twenty letters and a long manuscript for me; however, it is to my

Exhibit 7–1. The Value of Negotiation.

Source: Copyrighted illustrations by Eugene Mihaesco.

advantage to negotiate with her. I find that the manuscript is completed more cheerfully and with fewer errors if I walk into her office with the manuscript in one hand and the letters in the other, and I ask her if she is busy. Having observed the yellow handwritten piles in both hands, she predictably responds in the affirmative. I then say something like this: "Ok, then, I'll make you an offer you can't refuse. You type the manuscript, because accuracy is really important in it. And I'll have my grader type the letters."

Like most other ongoing exchange relationships, the negotiation process allows the parties to state their preferences and discuss their relationship before doing anything about it (Kelley & Schenitzki, 1972). Negotiation allows the parties to maintain contact with each other and gather information about the other (Iklé, 1964). Most importantly, it gives the parties time to think.

The negotiated agreement itself offers assets, because it constrains the opponent's current and future moves. As a colleague once noted, negotiation serves as a minefield in reducing the probability that the opponent will approach from a certain direction. Although the agreement probably does not constrain the opponent as effectively as a minefield, it does increase predictability, so the opponent is not a "loose cannon." It cuts off some avenues of competition, and in so doing it underpins future harmonious relationships. For example, the SALT II pact attempted to provide these functions. To eliminate some avenues of competition, it stated that the United States and the Soviet Union would no longer compete in terms of numbers of strategic weapons (land vehicles or silos, submarine tubes, heavy intercontinental bombers, and cruise-carrying bombers). Some quality constraints also were agreed upon: each side could develop only one "new-type" missile. Other avenues were left open: improvements could be made in submarine-launched missiles; U.S. medium-range weapons deployed in Europe could be increased and improved; and medium-range Soviet bombers were in no way constrained ("Soviet Government," 1979).

Although the negotiation process and agreement have their assets, they also are plagued with liabilities. Perhaps the most salient is time. Negotiations, be they tacit or explicit, consume time. It might be argued that in the long run a negotiation is time effective in that it reduces the time consumed by conflict, poorly coordinated activities, poor decision making, and deadlocked exchanges. In the short run, however, negotiation requires an investment of time; the SALT II negotiations and the Camp David "agreement" took years of negotiation. Likewise, pelt traders can negotiate for an hour over one skin.

A cost that proves more dysfunctional to the negotiator than time is the appearance of weakness. A negotiator's willingness and offer to negotiate an issue is perceived by the constituent, opponent, and negotiator as an admission that methods for better controlling the exchange are unavailable to the negotiator. Managers, for example, may hesitate to negotiate with a subordinate because they have at their disposal many power sources—legitimate and interpersonal—that they can utilize. Furthermore, managers know that negotiating with a subordinate indicates that they do not have the power to prescribe the subordinate's behavior. Likewise, lawyers in pretrial conferences are extremely hesitant to indicate their willingness to negotiate a settlement, because they fear such an overture will be perceived by both the opponent and the judge as an indication of a weak case. Thereby, in almost all conferences the judge must be the first to suggest a negotiation.

A willingness to negotiate implies weakness not only to the negotiator and opponent, but also to the negotiator's constituent. It gives the appearance that the negotiator is incapable of or unwilling to take charge of the situation. An interesting example of such a case occurred in the Carter administration during the latter months of 1979. In March of that year, President Jimmy Carter decided to appoint Robert Strauss, a lawyer-politician and trade negotiator, as a special envoy to the Middle East. Shortly thereafter, the president notified National Security Advisor Zbigniew Brzezinski that he wanted Strauss's role enlarged so that he could better maintain the primary responsibility of dealing with Israeli Prime Minister Menachem Begin and Egyptian President Anwar as-Sadat.

Upon learning the news, Secretary of State Cyrus Vance threatened resignation. In the forthcoming negotiation among Vance, Strauss, Hamilton Jordan (representing Carter), and Vice-President Walter Mondale (serving as the mediator), Vance argued that he would resign because the move would entail a "terrible blow for the State Department." At first he refused to budge, but later in the night he negotiated an agreement and did not resign. However, as a close friend put it, "He was humiliated by it." And he remained dispirited for months ("Who Conceded," 1979).

Vance had negotiated because of his loyalty to the president and the government. However, it was later reported that it was Vance's very willingness to negotiate that eventually lowered Carter's high opinion of his secretary of state. Ironically, Carter soon was to fall victim to the same curse; experts seem to agree that he would have won the 1980 election if he had attacked Iran instead of negotiating with its leaders.

A related cost of negotiation is to be found in the effects negotiations have on third parties observing the negotiations. In general, a negotiation alters their expectations for their future dealing with the negotiator. Specifically, negotiators who bargain with and make major concessions to their opponents will be expected by third parties to yield in a similar fashion whenever they deal with the third parties.

This cost was the major fear of the Polish regime during the September 1980 shipyard strikes. Knowing that all Polish workers were observing its handling of the strike, the government meticulously considered how each move would subsequently affect its relationship with the other workers. It feared that negotiating with the strikers (which it did) would engender further strikes (which it did) in other parts of Poland. And the government knew that yielding major concessions (which it did) would raise the expectations of other workers (which it did) that they be given equal or better concessions in any forthcoming exchanges. Finally, after entering into and hammering out an agreement with the strikers and thereby raising the expectations of others, the party boss was replaced. His negotiation had cost him not only future negotiation difficulties, but also the loss of confidence from his superiors in Moscow.

Finally, we must note that negotiating or attempting to negotiate with the opponent can expose the negotiator to physical harm. Many a soldier has been shot down carrying a white flag, and Rudolf Hess, at the time of this writing, still sits in Spandau prison regretting his attempt to negotiate a peace treaty between England and Germany.

Organizational Negotiation

Most writers discuss negotiation as it applies to conflict resolution. Such a perspective shortchanges the process, for as we will see, the applicability of negotiation extends beyond conflict resolution into the arenas of decision making, group management, turnover reduction, and group integration. These latter applications occur principally within the organization; therefore, before pursuing each in detail, it is useful to consider the general role played by negotiations in this locale.

Individuals within an organization find themselves in exchange relationships with groups and other individuals, and to a large extent their behavior in these relationships is controlled by rules, customs, norms, structures, and technological constraints. A telephone repairer, for instance, arrives at work at seven in the morning, because this is the appointed starting time. As is the custom in her unit, she chats over coffee for fifteen minutes before checking her truck. A co-worker who has helped her in the past finds that she has drawn several difficult assignments for that day, so the repairer works hard to complete her rounds and then assists the co-worker in hers. In "running down" a particularly difficult outage, the repairer works her way back from the receiver to the patchbox to the line to the main circuit to the home station, as the technology dictates.

However, rules and norms are not sufficient, precise, complex, or flexible enough to govern all personal behavior and relationships. Some "exceptions" can be handled by managerial or personal dictates or by persuasion. Many, however—especially the more novel ones—are left to interpersonal bargaining. For example, when new uniforms arrive for the telephone repairers, the question of the disposal of the old uniforms always arises. Managerial preference leans toward requiring that the old uniforms be turned in, whereas the employees favor their retention by each employee. Some interesting tacit arrangement usually is struck: the management requires that all old uniforms be turned in but allows each person to "lose" one-half the old uniforms.

It is also important to note that many of the rules, norms, customs, structures, and technologies we assume to be "established" were at one time established via tacit negotiating, explicit negotiating, or both. Furthermore, all of these have temporal limits; they will be reviewed, reevaluated, changed, or renewed in the future, as they were in the past (Strauss, 1978). For instance, the twelve-hour workday was once considered the rule within organizations. This was reviewed and modified to a ten- and then eight-hour day; concomitantly, the accepted six-day workweek was trimmed to five days. As we observe today, these agreements are submitted to constant review and modification. Likewise, hot type was considered the rule in the newspaper industry; it later was scrutinized by management and, after lengthy negotiation, replaced by cold type.

Like the rules themselves, compliance to them usually is negotiated. Note, for example, that in every hospital, rules and customs prescribe which procedures and treatments are to be handled by physicians and which are to be handled by nurses. In many hospitals, however, physicians allow nurses to administer treatments, and they teach many of them diagnostic techniques in exchange for their increased assistance in overload conditions. Similarly, plant rules within production facilities dictate employee hours, smoking breaks, personal time, days off, vacations, and so on. However, supervisors allow "good" workers to punch out early, take excessive smoking breaks, and in many other ways to trade their good performance for reduced prescriptions and proscriptions concerning their behavior.

In the legal realm, similar variances in compliance exist. The law in many states prohibits judges in settlement proceedings from offering a settlement figure to attorneys, putting pressure on attorneys to accept such a figure, or interviewing one attorney in the absence of the other. However, judges engage in these practices. Attorneys permit them to do so by failing to appeal such actions, and the infringements consequently underpin a large percentage of out-of-court settlements.

The negotiation processes previously discussed, although omnipresent in the organization, are infrequently salient to even an astute bystander. The negotiation endemic to decision making and other leadership activities is more frequently recognized.

Role of Negotiation in Decision Making

In discussing the role of negotiation in decision making, bear in mind first that negotiation is not a type of decision making, and decision making is not a type of negotiation. The processes can and frequently are independent—people can make decisions without negotiating, and they can negotiate without making decisions. Note also that whenever the processes are interdependent, the causation can travel in either direction. Consider the following relationship: negotiation = f(decision making). The chapter on strategy, Chapter 5, showed that decision making is a major determinant of effective negotiation; that is, negotiators must consider the situation, their own goals, and the tactics and maneuvers at their disposal, and then make decisions about how they will negotiate.

Consider also the opposite directional causation—the one of principal interest to us here—decision making = f(negotiation). Perhaps this is not as intuitively clear at this point; therefore, we first will clarify the impact negotiation has on the individual and group decision making processes and then consider some of the factors promoting or enhancing the effects of negotiations in decision making.

As a preface to this discussion, let us examine the decision-making process. It is a set of activities or subprocesses that results in a choice from among available alternatives. Its subprocesses are as follows:

1. Disequilibrium (recognition that a decision needs to be made).
2. Analysis of the situation.
3. Establishment and ranking of the criteria for choosing among the alternatives.
4. Identification of alternative courses of action.
5. Assessment of the consequences of each alternative and the probability of each consequence.
6. Consideration of the alternatives and consequences in light of the selected criteria and thereby the choice of the alternatives.
7. Application of the criteria to the alternatives.

Entwined with these steps is another: search behavior. At any point,decision makers may engage in search behavior. No doubt they will search for information once they recognize that a decision is necessary. As they analyze the situation, they might seek information concerning what the appropriate criteria are for such a decision. Likewise, most decision makers explore the alternatives open to them, gleaning information about the probable consequences of each alternative.

It can be argued that every decision involving more than one party entails some negotiation unless a large power differential exists between the parties. Consider first the case of individual decision making in which the decision maker interacts with at least one other.

Individual Decision Making

Initially, the decision maker realizes that a decision must be made or that opportunities are afforded for decision making. He analyzes the decision, identifies his alternatives, and establishes some criteria for choosing among them. If the decision maker alone can carry out these and the subsequent activities, no negotiation is required. However, if he is dependent upon another for decision analysis, alternative identification, or criteria establishment, then tacit or explicit negotiation is in the works. Outside parties seldom supply these services free of charge. Perhaps the decision maker can use persuasion to obtain such assistance, convincing the other that the assistance will yield outcomes that are desirable. If the decision maker holds the advantage, he can use a power play to gain assistance. In most cases, though, the decision maker finds that persuasion is ineffective and that he has little power over the other. Thus, he must proffer outcomes to the other in exchange for aid and tacitly or explicitly negotiate an acceptable rate of exchange.

Having identified his alternatives and chosen his criteria, the decision maker assesses the consequences of each alternative, again probably engaging in some search behavior. If the search is conducted in isolation from others, no negotiation is necessary. If the decision maker must acquire information from others, however, he again encounters questions about the price to be paid for their services. Similarly, if the decision maker alone makes the choice among the alternatives, he finds no negotiation necessary; as he involves another, however, he must consider that party's preferences, demands, expectations, and so on and then determine how much weight he will or must give to them. In sum, the individual decision maker's reliance on outside assistance or upon a fellow decision maker brings with it an exchange relationship and thereby the requirements for a minimum amount of negotiation.

Negotiation is required of the decision maker in several other instances. On occasion, some criteria by which he is to judge the alternatives are set externally, and he must first bargain to modify the criteria. For instance, in deciding upon the best tank design, a U.S. tank producer finds the tank cannot weigh more than sixty tons, because the Air Force planes cannot carry a larger tank. The tank producer thus makes decisions bound by the sixty-ton criterion or can attempt to modify this criterion by negotiating with the Air Force to build a fleet of planes capable of hauling seventy-ton tanks.

Negotiation also might be necessary to alter the available alternatives. For example, an associate was told by his boss to select two schools from among the ten top engineering schools in the United States for on-site interviews. The subordinate felt, given the high demand for engineers, that the top twenty schools should be considered as alternatives. Thus, he found his decision making highly dependent upon his negotiation over the number of alternative schools to be considered.

Time constraints, alternative consequences, problem areas, and other factors often force the individual decision maker to negotiate prior to, during, and after decision making. However, negotiation becomes more integral to decision making as groups make decisions.

Group Decision Making

An inertia exists within groups; they are somewhat slow to recognize or admit that a problem or opportunity exists that requires a decision. Consequently, the group member who perceives a problem or opportunity at times must convince associates of its existence. If the perceptive member's logic should fail, she then finds she must resort to other influence strategies such as persuasion, power, or negotiation.

After recognizing the need to make a decision and embarking upon the journey, the group typically embraces some forms of negotiated decision making. Questions arise about the necessity of an analysis, the thoroughness of the analysis, the amount of search activity to be employed, the type of search and analysis, and the temporal boundary of the search and analysis. Within the group there is seldom consensus about the answers to these questions. To formulate some acceptable level of consensus, members turn to logic, persuasion, trades, votes, arguments, or threats—that is, to a plethora of influence attempts (and among them, negotiation).

After analyzing the problem, the group concomitantly chooses criteria and sorts among alternatives. Disagreement arises in no small measure over various issues: the number of criteria, the relevance of the criteria, their ranking, the way in which criteria are to be combined, the number of alternatives, the relevant features of the alternatives, the sequence in which the alternatives are to be considered, and the type and extent of search behavior for unearthing new alternatives. As Maier (1973) points out, such disagreement has its assets and liabilities; the major liability is a deadlock. The techniques for averting or resolving deadlocks include those previously cited: votes, logic, persuasion, threats, power, arguments, haggling, murder, and negotiation. Negotiation is not the only consensus builder, nor in most cases is it the best. In many cases it is used, however, and it serves as an excellent fallback for the other techniques.

As the decision makers assess the consequences of the alternatives and use the criteria to select the most appropriate alternative, negotiation plays an increasingly important role. At times it replaces judgment as the method for assessing the alternatives. Group members trade on issues and reach compromises among their preferences as they strive to be accommodators who do not "rock the boat." Within the unit the members sacrifice, negotiating more tacitly than explicitly as they seek agreement on an item that meets a minimum level of acceptable criteria.

Upon the decision implementation, negotiation becomes more salient. Here the group must determine who is to implement the decision, that is, who is to make the additional inputs. Agreement must be struck somewhat simultaneously over the division of any outcomes accruing from the implementation. A negotiation thereby typically unfolds, because the members who invested high inputs into the decision making and implementation argue and bargain for the lion's share of the outcomes, whereas others employ various influence, arguments, maneuvers, and tactics to make a case for their own remuneration.

The preceding discussion concentrated on negotiation that evolves within the group as it makes decisions. As noted in reference to individual decision making, negotiation also takes place with outsiders. The group, in its search for alternatives, criteria, and information relevant to the decision, will find that it is reliant upon others for assistance. The amount of this assistance, the price at which it is extended, and the frequency at which it is to be provided are issues the group must hammer out in a tacit or explicit negotiation.

In summary, it has been argued that individuals and groups employ negotiation as they make decisions. Individuals find it useful in the procurement of information, assistance, and relaxed constraints from outsiders. Negotiation also serves such purposes for groups, but it also facilitates agreement and consensus building within them. Under some circumstances, both individual and group decision makers find negotiations entering into, facilitating, or impinging upon their decision making. An interesting question of both theoretical and practical interest that arises in reflection upon the negotiation–decision-making interplay is, What factors or contingencies promote negotiation within the decision-making process?

Factors Promoting Negotiation

Power does not promote negotiation; in fact, the opposite is the case. The more power decision makers have vis-à-vis fellow decision makers and those on whom they are dependent, the less likely they are to negotiate. Although the use of power is costly, it is less expensive than negotiation. Negotiation entails yielding an item—a cost to the decision maker—for the outcome received (cooperation, information, assistance, acceptance of a criterion, rejection of an alternative, and so on). Power does not entail this; it usually entails only diminished potency for future application.

Uncertainty has the opposite effect: the more uncertain the situation and thus the decision maker, the more likely she is to negotiate. Whenever the negotiator encounters uncertainty, she is less sure that her decision making will lead to the correct alternative; that is, she perceives a higher risk of failure. Negotiation allows the decision maker to spread the risk. Those within or external to her group who are allowed to influence the decision via the negotiation concomitantly assume some responsibility for the decision results.

President Ronald Reagan's decision concerning the sale of AWAC planes to Saudi Arabia in the fall of 1981 provides a signal example. There was a great deal of uncertainty in this case. The Saudis could use the planes against Israel, but the Saudis wanted the planes and hinted that relations with the United States hung in the balance. However, there was doubt that the planes were useful to the Saudi Arabian government, because their threats were more internal than external. Moshe Dayan, former defense minister of Israel, warned that Israel would blow the planes out of the sky if they collected air intelligence on Israel. Prime Minister Menachem Begin visited the United States to argue his case. The U.S. Senate was divided about fifty-fifty.

Given this uncertainty, Reagan negotiated. In the negotiations with the Saudis, he sought guarantees that if the planes were sold to them, they would not be used against Israel but instead would be deployed to effect a general stability of the entire area. In negotiations with the Israelis, he sought assurances that if the planes were not sold to the Saudis, Israel would act more responsibly in the area and would not for any reason attack or embarrass Saudi Arabia. Both the Saudis and Israelis used some of their chips, and a negotiated decision seemed to be struck: The United States would sell the AWACs to Saudi Arabia with the "expectation" that they would not be used against Israel, and the United States and Israel would engage in joint military ventures in the Middle East, plus Israel would receive "relevant" spy satellite data.

In this incident a decision maker, who was operating under uncertainty, was engaging in negotiations and allowing outsiders a chance to alter the decision. In exchange for the acceptance of their inputs, however, these outsiders had to assume some responsibility for the decision outcomes.

The effects of uncertainty also interact with the visibility of the decision results. Whenever the results will be highly visible, the decision makers' inclination to negotiate with those around them in the uncertain (versus certain) situation is quite high. In contrast, if the results are not to be visible, decision makers realize that their failures—more likely to be brought on by the uncertain situation—will be less damaging or embarrassing, and thus their propensity to negotiate responsibility in the face of uncertainty (versus certainty) is less than in the visible condition.

Visibility of the decision results, in addition to producing interactive effects, has an important effect in the decision maker's bargaining propensity. In general, negotiators are more likely to negotiate with fellow decision makers and outsiders when their decision results will be visible. They wish to spread the risk of any embarrassing (visible) failure—a risk that exists in even rather certain situations.

Another factor that can be expected to affect the decision maker's willingness to negotiate is the importance of the issue to be decided. Intuitively, we would argue that the more important the issue, the less likely the decision maker would be to negotiate. Negotiation typically brings with it certain compromises, and the decision maker does not wish to compromise on highly important items. This argument probably holds true for the decision maker's relationship with outsiders. If the decision is an important one, the decision maker wishes to hold the reins tightly and be exposed to limited outside influence.

The argument does not hold true for the relationship with fellow decision makers; this factor interacts with factors such as situation certainty and group member competence. Consider first the interplay with certainty. Whenever the issue is highly important and the decision maker very certain about the situation, he will make the decision. He knows what to do and does not wish to jeopardize an important issue through negotiation. However, if the issue is unimportant and the decision maker is very certain of his situation and decision, he will engage in a moderate amount of negotiation. Here he feels that the importance of the issue is low enough that any compromising via negotiation is of little concern. He also no doubt feels that negotiation and compromise on this issue probably yield him chips he can pocket for more important issues.

Turning to the low certainty condition, we note that whenever the decision maker faces a highly important issue, he is quite willing to negotiate. His willingness hinges on his understandable preference not to be solely responsible for making highly important decisions when the chances of a mistake are high. When the issue is of low importance, in contrast, the decision maker is ambivalent. He is not sure whether or not his decision will be the correct one, but the issue is unimportant, so the decision maker does not mind being held accountable.

A factor that interacts similarly with the issue importance is the capability of the decision maker's peers. It produces a strong main effect on its own: a decision maker is more willing to negotiate her decision making with capable peers than with those housing more feeble facilities. And this issue importance–peer capability interaction parallels the one previously discussed. Whenever the issue is highly important and the capabilities of compatriots is low, the decision maker does not negotiate. She makes the decision because she knows what to do and does not wish to jeopardize the decision by throwing it into the turnip patch. However, if the issue is of low importance and the capabilities of the fellows is also low, the decision maker is willing to negotiate in spite of her superior capabilities. Little is to be lost on an unimportant issue, and negotiating here might yield some chips for later use.

The decision maker with capable associates is very willing to negotiate on an important issue. She picks up useful assistance here and shares any risk of bungling the important issue. Whenever the issue is of low importance and the comrades are capable, the decision maker has a moderate to high incentive to negotiate. The group members are capable, so the decision maker is willing to have them exert influence through negotiation. However, she does not feel highly pressured to obtain their capable inputs, because the issue is not the most highly valued.

Negotiation strongly affects decision making in the organization, as we have seen. It also is applicable within other processes, notably those involving leadership.

Role of Negotiation in Leadership

For years leadership researchers have maintained that negotiation is one of the signal leadership functions. Specifically, Sayles (1964) believes negotiation is one of the most important parts of the manager's activity set. Mintzberg (1973) claims that the negotiator role is one of the ten a leader must perform in managing an organization. However, when scholars speak of leader negotiation, they focus primarily on external relationships; they perceive the leader's negotiation to revolve around negotiations with persons, groups, and institutions that supply goods and services to the leader's group. Likewise, leaders negotiate to set standards for outsiders' work, purchase their assistance, and control their activities. Admittedly, leaders spend considerable time and effort in conducting these negotiations, and their groups' successes are no doubt dependent upon their adroitness in the arena. However, a group's effectiveness, like that of its leader, also hinges strongly upon the leader's effectiveness in negotiations with subordinates.

Negotiations with Subordinates

Graen and his associates (Dansereau, Graen, & Haga, 1975; Graen, Dansereau, Haga, & Cashmen, 1975; Haga, Graen, & Dansereau, 1974) initiated the first studies of leader negotiation within the work group. Their findings reveal that the leader-subordinate dyads within groups can be divided into in-group and out-group categories. Specifically, the in-group relationship between leader and subordinates is one of negotiation. The subordinates receive latitude in developing their roles, inside information, influence in decision making, support for their actions, and consideration for their feelings in exchange for their strong involvement in administration and behavior consistent with their leader's expectations. In the out-group relationship, the superior does not negotiate. He supervises subordinates, relying primarily on his authority.

Looking more closely at the in-group, or negotiated, relationship, we note that leaders have sufficient valued outcomes at their disposal—salary increases, promotions, task assignments (which vary in difficulty, visibility, frustration, potential, and challenge), information, support, members' protection, and extent of participation in decision making—that they can exchange with subordinates. The subordinates can respond with extensive expenditures of time and energy; commitment to the organization; willingness to assume risk or responsibility; and, in general, assistance to superiors in their endeavors. When superiors choose to establish the negotiated relationship, they and their subordinates exchange their wares, tacitly hammering out agreements about which services will be exchanged and the rates of exchanges. Emanating from this negotiated relationship are higher performance ratings for the subordinates, more positive work attitudes by them, stronger loyalty to superiors, greater openness to others' ideas, and stronger trust within the dyad.

Whenever a superior chooses not to negotiate with some employees—placing them in the out-group—and relies principally upon his power, the relationship is more strained. Subordinates are not as loyal to the superior, trust him less, assume less risk, make fewer commitments to him, assume less responsibility, and so on.

Whereas Graen's description of the leadership process indicates the value of establishing and using a negotiation relationship with subordinates, it also suggests the value of effective leadership negotiation. Many of the worker performances desired by leaders—for example, performance above standard, finding better ways to perform a task, cooperation, and agreeableness with peers—cannot be obtained through the use of legitimate power, remuneration, promotion, or persuasion. A more malleable subordinate-superior exchange activity, such as negotiation, is needed, and the better leaders are at establishing, conducting, and implementing these negotiations, the more effective they will be.

For instance, consider leadership negotiation in the less-than-amorous context. From the Graen works we conclude that the leaders who establish and conduct in-group, or negotiated, relationships with subordinates do so because they like the subordinates. Negotiation serves quite well in such cases; fortunately, it serves even better for subordinates with whom the superior has no affinity. With this latter group, power, persuasion, and rules prove to be weary tools: such subordinates react negatively to the use of power; persuasion does not work, because they do not share the leader's goals; and rules prove to be the bane of the leader's existence. When the leader tries to use them, the subordinates will follow them to the letter.

Enter negotiation. Admittedly, the leader demonstrates some weakness when negotiating. Subordinates seldom react negatively to negotiation, however, for it gives them a feeling of participation; they feel their interests are being considered. Occasionally, in tacit and explicit negotiation, they develop some appreciation for the leader's perspective. Furthermore, if the negotiation fails, power can be used as the backup.

In addition to yielding some advantages over the use of power, negotiation also has an advantage over the operant use of rewards for leaders. For them, reinforcement frequently degenerates into a "Do what I tell you, and I'll reward you" ritual. Negotiation, in contrast, requires consideration of the subordinates' needs, aspirations, ideas, and utilities (values they place upon items) so that they can be moved, directed, or constrained as the leader desires.

In addition to being useful to leaders in administering rewards and gaining compliance, negotiation also assists them in setting goals with subordinates and enhancing their performance through the Management by Objectives (MBO) process.

Management by Objectives (MBO)

Management by Objectives is perhaps the best-known technique used by leaders to facilitate goal setting and accomplishment. It is generally conceded to be the brainchild of Peter F. Drucker (1954), who maintained that a leader's job requires him or her to balance the organization's needs and goals in every area in which the organization must perform effectively. Other scholars and practitioners have developed and refined the technique over the years such that today the process assumes the following format (Raio, 1974): (1) goal setting, (2) action planning, (3) self-control, and (4) periodic reviews.

At the heart of MBO lies goal setting. Having learned of the organizational goals, top managers develop their specific objectives. These are cleared with their superiors and then communicated to subordinates, who in turn develop goals and establish plans so that their goals, once implemented, facilitate those of their superiors and thereby the organizational objectives. In establishing objectives, managers find they must negotiate with both their superiors and subordinates. In negotiating with superiors, managers must win their approval of the selected objectives; in negotiating with subordinates, managers must ensure that the objectives of subordinates facilitate the accomplishment of the managers' own goals.

In setting goals, all managers, as well as their superiors and subordinates, are charged with setting objectives that are challenging, attainable, measurable, and relevant. As Raio (1974) notes, the goals should be challenging in that they should "stretch" each party. They should be somewhat difficult to achieve and should not contain excessive cushioning. However, they should be realistic and achievable, not too risky, and consistent with the person's capabilities and the support available. The objectives must be as specific and as quantitative as possible (measurable). Verification also must be considered: what data are needed and available to monitor progress. The measures must be reasonable, and the time intervals for evaluations must be acceptable. The objectives should be relevant—consistent with and complementary to the higher and organizational goals. They must serve valued functions for those who are dependent upon the goal setter.

What implications do these criteria hold for leaders? In short, they dictate that leaders set goals for themselves that they can attain and be rewarded for attaining. Leaders also must make sure that their superiors do not set goals that generate unrealistic demands for the leaders themselves. In all cases, leaders must make sure that their subordinates' goals underpin their own. Given these multiple and often conflicting goals, how do leaders proceed?

Leaders negotiate. In interacting with their superiors, leaders seek primarily an approval of somewhat low, attainable goals plus assurances that suitable rewards (outcomes) will be forthcoming from their attainment. Superiors, however, seek and demand higher goals—those that are challenging—for they are more likely to ensure their own goal accomplishment and rewards. Thus, superiors strive to commit leaders to higher goals, express doubts as to whether the proffered goals are sufficiently "motivating," hold that the goals are not relevant, argue that measurement, etc. will be a problem, and tender low rewards and commitments for such "insufficient aspirations." Leaders counter, defending their objectives, and raising them somewhat in exchange for the superiors' approval or promises to reward their attainment. Simultaneously, leaders communicate with those below to determine if they can help meet the new objectives, and they negotiate to gain their commitments, using ploys similar to those of superiors.

As leaders negotiate with the subordinates, they seek not only high goals, but also a commitment to high-level performance. They wish for the subordinates' goals to be attainable, because an excessive, unattainable goal would serve more as a bad joke than as a challenging adventure. Therefore, leaders at times are willing to concede to subordinates, allowing them to lower their goals. Leaders also bargain quite specifically for measurable goals, because they simplify their future exchanges with subordinates and allow leaders greater leverage in controlling the subordinates' performance.

As the implementation of MBO requires leaders to negotiate with both superiors and subordinates in the goal-setting phase, it at the same time permanently alters the superior-leader and leader-subordinate relationships. These relationships, consultants report, become negotiated orders (Strauss, 1978). Such an observation is admittedly counterintuitive, for it seems that once the leader's (or subordinate's) objectives have been hammered out, reduced to writing, reviewed by the superior, and signed as an agreement, the relationship would be fixed. However, observations reveal that the MBO agreement and the process whereby it was established open the door for ongoing negotiations within the hierarchy.

Circumstances often arise such that a leader of subordinate cannot meet objectives. For instance, a car salesperson commits herself to increasing her sales by 30 percent, but interest rates jump five points in that period. Is the subordinate held to the MBO contract? Subordinates seldom are; usually a round of negotiations will ensure over a new goal and the rewards to be forthcoming at its accomplishment.

Continued negotiations are not engendered solely from the bottom of the organization. After MBO agreements have been struck up and down the hierarchy, the company goals and strategies might require immediate modification, and many of the old agreements become irrelevant or require modification. Consider the ramifications of a product line conversion. The old MBO agreement perhaps called for a 3 percent defect rate on the old product line items (items that had been produced for years, so all workers were skilled at their tasks). Is the production manager to be held to the 3 percent defect rate for the new products? Probably not: There are too many new questions; uncertainties will arise in the production; and many people on the line will be pushed back on their learning curve.

External changes, new decisions by management, changes integral to the organization, new helpful information, and changing attitudes all require tacit, if not specific, modification of the MBO accord. However, the most amusing need for modifications comes from new managers. In their first few rounds through the MBO process new managers, in an attempt to impress their bosses, usually promise more than they can deliver in the forthcoming year. As the months roll by it becomes painfully obvious that the goals are not attainable. Negotiation—preferably instituted by a superior—can serve here as a potential exit from a novice's embarrassment.

Turnover Reduction

Effective negotiation, in addition to assisting leaders in implementing MBO programs, also can reduce turnover in their ranks. It does so via three routes: (1) The leader's willingness to negotiate and his active negotiation with subordinates reduces the subordinates' turnover; (2)

the leader's effective negotiation eliminates, reduces, or mitigates many of the causes of subordinate turnover; and (3) the leader's willingness and capability to negotiate on the behalf of subordinates reduces their voluntary terminations.

Consider the effect of turnover within each route. Graen's works, as noted previously, unearthed two types of leader-subordinate dyads: the in-group, or negotiated, dyad and the out-group dyad. When the leader established a negotiation relationship with the subordinates, the subordinates were more committed to the organization and more satisfied with the organization and the leader. Consider these observations in conjunction with the reported findings of Porter, Crampon, and Smith (1976), Steers (1977), and others that high commitment to the organization reduces turnover. Also think about these observations in light of a host of studies (see Mobley, Griffeth, Hand, & Meglino, 1979, for an excellent review) showing that satisfied workers quit less often. Given these two sets of observations—(1) that negotiations with subordinates result in subordinate commitment and satisfaction and (2) that this commitment and satisfaction result in low turnover—we logically can deduce that negotiating with subordinates reduces their turnover.

In the second route through which leader negotiation reduces turnover—elimination of the causes of turnover—we note that the primary factors affecting turnover are age, tenure, intentions to remain on the job, overall satisfaction, job content, and commitment (Mobley, Griffeth, Hand, & Meglino, 1979). Although leader negotiation probably can have little effect on the first three factors, it seems plausible that it could alter the latter three and thereby reduce turnover. Consider first the enhancement of overall satisfaction.

As noted previously, leader negotiations with subordinates raise their satisfaction, probably because the subordinates appreciate the give-and-take interaction with the leader and enjoy the rewards flowing from it. Satisfaction also can be enhanced by the effect of negotiation on the subordinates' CL. Recall that the subordinates' satisfaction is a function of the difference between their CLs (NOs they feel they deserve from the organization) and the NOs they receive. Therefore, subordinate satisfaction will rise if the subordinates' CLs can be reduced.

Reduction of the CL is a major function of negotiations. As previous chapters noted, a negotiator can use a plethora of tactics to reduce the opponent's CL; the same tactics are available to the leader in dealing with subordinates. For instance, a leader can complain that subordinates expect or demand too much, delay until the subordinates' position weakens, withhold relevant information from subordinates, bias information, demand that subordinates state their goals, or threaten to fire them.

Probably, though, a leader can expect more leverage upon the subordinates' satisfaction by negotiating to raise their NOs (rewards). Of the immense body of material written and assembled about the causes of satisfaction, most supports the proposition that rewards lead to satisfaction. Leaders can use their negotiations to enhance both forms of subordinate rewards: intrinsic and extrinsic.

Perhaps surprisingly, negotiation is more effective in raising intrinsic rewards (those inherent to the task). A task and its completion are more (intrinsically) satisfying to subordinates if they receive enough help and equipment to complete the job, have enough information to get the job done, possess enough authority to do the job, have the opportunities to develop special abilities, and have adequate time to complete the task (Quinn et al., 1971). These job facets do not simply exist or materialize magically; they must be provided. Leaders can supply some themselves, but most require assistance from and negotiation with superiors and managerial colleagues. For instance, necessary equipment owned and controlled by other departments at times must be acquired through a leader's interaction with another department head. This department head's acquiescence will not be without some cost and haggling—tacit or explicit—over the cost. The leader can grant some authority to complete the job to a subordinate, but authority to control goods and services in other areas must be acquired via bargaining, persuasion, or other acceptable ploys. As any manager in a mechanistic production system knows, freeing up time for a subordinate to do a job requires haggling or striking some bargain with the leader's superior, industrial engineers, or managers up and down the production line.

The leader's interaction—negotiations, persuasions, and politicing—with outsiders also raises subordinate satisfaction by ensuring that the subordinate has sufficient supplies to complete the task. Likewise, this interaction ensures that interruptions from maintenance staff, custodians, and demand aberrations are minimized. For example, a cause of significant dissatisfaction in the warp production departments of textile mills is the termination of the workday. On occasion, demand for cloth slackens, inventories of warped thread fill, and top managers terminate a shift at seemingly arbitrary times. In such cases, a leader's negotiation can greatly reduce worker dissatisfaction. The leader can negotiate for shifts into other production lines, slow or spread production over several days, schedule interruptions on preferred days (such as the opening day of rabbit season), or at least procure accurate predictions about when the interruptions will occur. Finally, a leader's negotiations can ensure not only that subordinates' tasks remain uninterrupted, but also that the demands made upon their production do not vary excessively.

The extrinsic component of subordinate rewards also can be improved with leader negotiation. However, the usefulness of negotiation in this arena is somewhat more limited. Consider first some basics. Subordinates are more likely to be satisfied when their extrinsic rewards are high, and when these rewards closely follow and correlate positively with the subordinates' behavior and goal accomplishments. By negotiating, usually vertically, leaders at times can obtain higher rewards for subordinates. For instance, they can guarantee or promise that increased productivity or reduced turnover will accrue from the increased funding; they can pessimistically predict the opposite if rewards are not increased; or they can proffer enhanced loyalty and considerations to be named later.

Once the rewards have been negotiated from external sources, they should be administered on a contingent basis; there should be no negotiation here. In general, satisfaction will be high in the absence of negotiation. Subordinates will perform, be rewarded, and be satisfied with a reward that is fair. In the administration of rewards, negotiation would simply engender difficulties. First, it would raise the subordinates' aspirations. Second, it would raise questions as to whether or not rewards are to be contingently administered. Finally, current norms in hierarchical organizations preclude negotiations as an acceptable method for determining subordinate remuneration.

Although negotiations should not enter into a leader's routine administration of rewards, it should be used for exceptions. In such cases, if rules, norms, or precedents do not determine how the rewards are to be administered, discussion and negotiation with subordinates can allow them to participate in establishing the criteria by which rewards are determined.

Having examined the role played by leader negotiation with subordinates and by leader negotiations to eliminate the causes of turnover, we now turn to the effect of the leader's willingness and capability to negotiate on the behalf of subordinates. The leader's participation in such negotiations has a tandem effect on turnover. The first facet might best be labeled *public relations ploys.* Subordinates appreciate and are impressed by their leader's negotiation on their behalf. Be it over a minor rule infraction, a special privilege requested, or a major production alteration, a leader's representation of subordinates demonstrates loyalty, sensitivity, and commitment to them. The subordinates perceive this as a valued outcome in their job; wish to reciprocate such actions; develop strong allegiances to the leader; and, as a result, are less likely to depart.

The second facet is more substantive: a leader's representation of subordinates yields tangible outcomes to them. As Likert (1961) notes, a leader's upward negotiation makes the subordinates' opinions and interests more salient to superiors who are making decisions of wide impact. Conversely, a leader's upward negotiation provides a buffer for subordinates against the superiors' arbitrary decisions, and both the leader's horizontal and vertical negotiations protect the subordinates from encroachments and demands made by people of greater or equal power within several segments of the organization. Finally, the leader's negotiations coordinate the subordinates' activities with those of others with whom they are interdependent. Such coordination does not occur automatically. Interdependent groups in organizations usually pursue different goals. Thus, when left to their own means and motivations, members of different groups will fail to cooperate. As a result, they experience high levels of frustration and tension. The leader's negotiation helps align intergroup interests; facilitates subordinate satisfaction and productivity; and, in general, reduces the intragroup and intergroup tensions that result in turnover.

Organizational Integration

The chapter to this point has dealt with negotiation in the organization as a mechanism for facilitating decision making and assisting the leader in interaction with the group. In addition to underpinning these microprocesses, negotiation also assists organizational managers in their vertical and horizontal integration of different groups.

Horizontal Integration

Organizations, like groups, consist of interdependent parts that have their own values, interests, perceptions, and goals. Each unit seeks to fulfill its particular goal—Environmental Protection Agency (EPA) lawyers pursue their cases, surgeons operate, and newspaper reporters track down and write stories—and the effectiveness of the organization depends on the success of each unit's fulfillment of its specialized task. Just as important as the fulfillment of the separate tasks is the integration of the unit activities such that each unit's activities aid or at least do not conflict with those of the others. For example, the surgeon may need the assistance of a pathologist during an operation, the EPA lawyer may need information supplied by a toxicologist prior to a suit, or the reporter may need the editor's and photocopier's assistance after writing the story.

To integrate the functional units, the organization implements alternative organizing modes. Organizations that face rather simple tasks and stable environments use norms, authority, rules, and procedures to coordinate their units, whereas those facing more uncertainty because of more complex tasks and dynamic environments turn to planning, goal setting, and a narrowing span of control. As uncertainty increases, the number of exceptions requiring managerial attention also increases to the point where the hierarchy is overloaded. Thus, the organization must undertake additional or different integrative action. In this strategic choice, the organization can proceed in one or all of five directions: environmental management, creation of slack resources, creation of self-contained tasks, investment in vertical information systems, and creation of lateral relations (Galbraith, 1977). The first and last entail and require negotiation; environmental management will be discussed shortly and lateral relations, here.

Lateral relations allow decisions to be made horizontally across lines of authority. Such a process moves the level of decision making down to the point at which the information exists instead of bringing the information up the hierarchy for the decision to be made. Several mechanisms are employed.

The simplest and most often used lateral relation is direct negotiation between two persons who must coordinate their united activities. In most organizations these contacts are so prevalent that they seem routine. A project manager discusses problems with a design engineer; the firm's marketing supervisor discusses a need with a departmental production head; the chief surgeon asks a favor of a head nurse; and a Mideast expert in the State Department acquires information from a munitions expert in the Defense Department. As these examples reveal, not all these exchanges entail negotiations. A good many do, however, because the interacting parties coming from different groups and serving different subgoals have different perspectives and approaches (Dearborn & Simon, 1958). These differing goals and orientations quite frequently lead to impasses requiring negotiations.

In interunit negotiations, explicit trading often is observed. The production manager agrees to run overtime and produce a variety of items to reduce the marketing manager's "off-shelf" time if the marketing department will offer a large sale on one item so the production manager can schedule the production lines for a long run and thereby get the cost per unit down next month. Reporters agree to get their stories in earlier if the copy editors will agree to perform less surgery on them. At times the negotiation is more tacit, as when one production unit corrects the mistakes made by a former in exchange for the former's speeding up of the production sequence.

Regardless of whether these negotiations are tacit or explicit, they provide a useful function: they coordinate the units' activities and avoid upward referral and overload of a higher authority. They also focus the parties' attentions on the constraints and uncertainties under which they operate and force them to consider the effects of these phenomena. Such negotiations also force each side to better understand its own needs as well as its dependencies on its counterpart and enable or force each to understand the other's needs and points of view. This enhanced knowledge not only better facilitates any imminent coordination, but also sets the stage for longer-run coordination.

When there is frequent and substantial contact between two groups, such as between purchasing and production departments, a liaison role—a person or a team—often is created to handle the contacts. Liaisons act somewhat as mediators between members of the units. They seek to facilitate the interunit coordination in a variety of ways. At one extreme they do very little, simply passing or translating information from one side to the other. At the other extreme they dictate what the relationship will be. Usually liaisons operate between the extremes, negotiating with and seeking to alter the relationships among the unit members.

Vertical Integration

Negotiation not only facilitates horizontal coordination and integration in the organization; it also aids vertical integration. Just like horizontal groups, vertical groups differ significantly in their norms, values, and goals. Groups at the lowest levels of the hierarchy must be concerned with performing specific, specialized tasks. Moving up the hierarchy, the goals change. They are related to general tasks and to coordination of groups. At the higher levels, goals focus on a large overall task and the control and coordination of many functional groups. The differences in goals, values, perspectives, time horizons, and so on usually cause little difficulty, because the upper-level personnel use their power to handle the relationship with subordinates.

However, the use of power has its costs; therefore, the higher groups often negotiate with the lower.

As the complexity, as well as the dynamics, of the environment increase and the organization becomes more decentralized, the superiors find that the lower units are quite powerful and must be dealt with accordingly. Thus, the upper-level personnel negotiate with the subordinates. For example, President Richard Nixon, much to his dismay, found that he could not simply order the State Department officials to proceed in a certain manner. If they agreed with his decision, they would expedite an order. If they did not, they would drag their feet or claim that their hands were tied. Thus, the president found himself having to negotiate with lower-level units, agreeing to integrate their ideas into his decisions.

Coalitions

To this point the discussion of integration has concentrated on the role played by negotiations horizontally at the lower levels and vertically between the higher and lower levels. As Thompson (1967) points out, negotiations also play a signal role horizontally at the highest level. Organizations are seldom run by a single, all-powerful individual, because most organizations operate with imperfect technologies and in complex environments that preclude the use of simple one-person decision processes. Inputs from and cooperation with many units are necessary, and thus control and coordination of these units can be exercised only with some sort of coalition. The more numerous the complex units, the larger the coalition becomes and the more likely the organization is to form an inner coalition. In turn, the person who can control this inner coalition controls the organization.

Coalitions form because the powerful individuals from the various units will not subserve their unit's resources, time, and services to the "leader" unless a "representative" from their unit is allowed some influence in the organizational decision making and control. That is, they negotiate with the leader and the other powerful representatives concerning the condition under which they will cooperate with them in running the organization. Succinctly stated, these potential members of the dominant coalition tacitly and explicitly hammer out an agreement about the exchange that is to take place between them or their constituent group and the rest of the organization. Those with the most valued resources (for example, the capacity to manage an uncertain segment of the environment or the ability to operate a scarce and valuable technology) find it possible to glean substantial power. Those with less useful knowledge or less scarce resources must be satisfied with less power and at times find themselves shut out and ruled by the dominant coalition.

As a footnote to all this, whenever there is a wide distribution of power within the organization and thereby a large dominant coalition, an inner core must be formed to run the organization. Without this inner core, the organization would find itself highly constrained, if not paralyzed, in its operations. It continually would find the coalition divided into factions (lacking common goals) and thereby unable to come to an agreement or divided into subcoalitions (with common goals) and at loggerheads over various questions. To avoid these difficulties, the leader—via negotiations or use of power—must forge this inner coalition and keep it from dividing into factions over an excessive number of issues.

External Negotiations

The discussion of decision making, group leadership, and integration has focused on the application of negotiation to intraorganizational processes. However, negotiations probably are most frequently employed by organizations to handle their interactions with external or environmental entities. Organizations seldom have power over all outside entities; they infrequently share their goals; and, typically, they maintain perspectives different from those of organizations with whom they interact. Thus, power plays, persuasion, and joint decision making are less than viable, and the organization must fall back upon negotiations. For the sake of discussion, these negotiation interactions can be cleaved into two, although somewhat overlapping, spheres: the sustenance negotiations and the conflict resolution negotiations.

Sustenance Negotiations

Organizations, like all systems—persons, nations, amoebas, frogs, and so on—must acquire essential inputs to survive. Survival likewise depends on the organization's outputting various products, protecting itself from potentially harmful elements in the environment, and coordinating its activities with the other elements in the environment. Negotiation offers a means for obtaining these processes and a fair chance for reducing the cost of doing so.

Numerous examples validate the importance of negotiation for inputting: The Defense Department procures 90 percent of its requirements on a negotiated basis. Organizations negotiate with unions over the rates at which labor will be supplied. Smart administrators bargain with financial institutions over the rate at which capital will be supplied. Land prices usually are considered "negotiable."

Outputting in most cases is the mirrored reflection of inputting. Organizations negotiate with individuals and organizations in their environments over the terms at which products and services will be accepted. In many cases, this negotiation entails only one trial. For example, a construction firm enters one competitive bid to the city of Columbus, Ohio. If it is accepted, the city agrees to take the firm's product or service. Likewise, a restaurant engages in a take-it-or-leave-it negotiation with its potential clientele when it displays its menu.

In contrast, many outputting negotiations are multitrial. An organization offers an item in exchange for a stated price, and the potential recipient responds with an acceptance, counteroffer, or abandonment of the relationship. With an acceptance, the organization outputs its product. With a counteroffer, the negotiation continues. With a severing of the relationship, the organization begins the search for potential recipients.

Protection Negotiations • Perhaps not as salient to the layperson as the inputting and outputting negotiations are the negotiations the organization enters into for its own protection. Sometimes tacit agreements such as "live and let live" are struck, and these later evolve into norms or values for the related groups (Warren, Rose, & Bergunder, 1974). At times, such as with nonaggression treaties, they are quite explicit. Be they tacit or explicit, protection negotiations have the goal of forming a type of negotiated boundary around the organization's vital elements. As opposed to the goal of the inputting and outputting negotiations—insurance that sufficient and correct items flow through the boundary to sustain the organization—the goal of protection negotiations is to sustain the organization by ensuring that unwanted items do not flow through.

Coordination Negotiations • Finally, many negotiations the organization enters are aimed at coordinating its activities with those around it. In such negotiations the goal is to ensure that other organizations aid or at least do not damage the organization as it interacts with third parties. Such negotiations can center around joint ventures (the

Alaskan pipeline), price fixing (OPEC practices), or carving up conquered territories (the Allies' activities after World War II). They also can be entered to attack an opponent or protect the organization from an attack by an opponent (NATO and the Warsaw Pact agreements). They can ensure that one organization will do nothing while the other acts (the explicit Stalin-Hitler pact with regard to Poland or the implicit U.S.-Soviet pact that allowed the Soviets to seize the Balkans).

For the organization, coordination negotiations differ from those of the other sustenance negotiations (inputting, outputting, or protection) in one major respect. Those three focus upon insurance that the exchange with the other party will provide sufficient net benefits (that is, outcomes minus costs) from that party. In contrast, coordination negotiations seek to ensure that the organization's exchange or encounter with the third party will be maximally beneficial.

Conflict Resolution Negotiations

Like organizational sustenance negotiations, those that manage conflict are directed toward parties outside the organization. Conflict resolution negotiations also ensue at different levels within and outside the organization (for example, at the interpersonal, intragroup, and intergroup levels). Because of this latter phenomenon, the discussion of conflict resolution negotiations is applicable to many of these different levels.

Winston Churchill perhaps stated it best: "Jaw-jaw is better than war-war." Negotiation, to be sure, is quite useful when it substitutes for conflict, but its benefits are not limited to this realm. It also helps eliminate the causes of conflict; aids parties in coordinating their activities and thereby avoiding conflict whenever the causes cannot be eliminated; and, perhaps most importantly, leads to a better understanding of conflict for the interacting parties.

To get a better feel for the importance of negotiation in conflict management, we first need to focus on the conflict concept. Succinctly, *conflict* is a process in which two or more parties attempt to frustrate the other's goal attainment. There appears to be a general agreement that the factors underlying conflict are threefold (March & Simon, 1958): interdependence, differences in goals, and differences in perceptions (Exhibit 7–2).

Interdependence • Interdependence has as its primary cause a mutual dependence on limited resources. Seldom do people, groups,

Exhibit 7–2. Sources of Conflict.

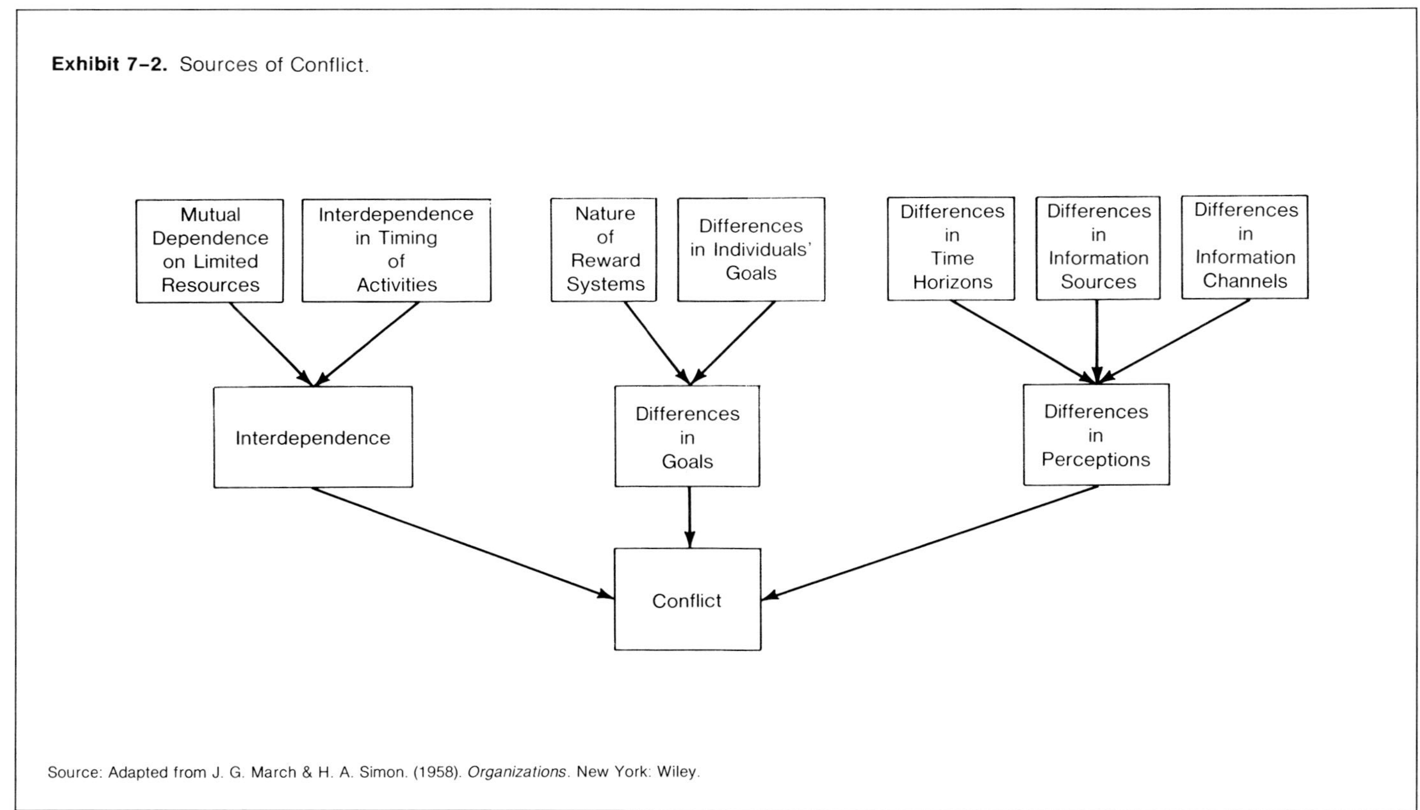

Source: Adapted from J. G. March & H. A. Simon. (1958). *Organizations*. New York: Wiley.

or organizations operate with unlimited resources in a munificent environment. Rather, they face limited resources because the environment is not munificent and because other entities—persons, groups, or organizations—also seek these environmental resources. As the mutual dependence upon the same resources increases—because of a drying up of resources, an increased number of parties striving for the resources, or both—so does competition for these resources and thereby the potential for conflict.

Another source of interdependence is the timing of activities, which can spawn two varieties: sequential and reciprocal interdependence (Thompson, 1967). In sequential interdependence, one party can complete its task only after the other has completed its task. The most common example of this interdependence is found on production lines. In the assembly of a television, for example, Assembler M can solder parts (transistors, resistors, chips, or whatever) to the plate only after Assembler L has positioned the various parts.

In contrast, reciprocal interdependence involves processes in which both parties in turn are dependent on the performance of the other. General Joseph W. Stilwell's ground forces in China during World War II found themselves in reciprocal interdependence with the Air Corps. The Air Corps brought in supplies, bombed Japanese targets, and on occasion provided close air support for the infantry. For its part, the infantry secured the airfields and provided sufficient land buffers between the enemy and the vulnerable landing fields, grounded airplanes, fuel depots, maintenance facilities, and munition storages.

Although both forms of interdependence are intended to benefit one or both of the interdependent parties, the interdependence also contributes to conflict between them. Each party has as its goal the completion of its particular task (for example, soldering a plate or transporting supplies). If the other party frustrates or delays this goal by failing to complete its necessary facet, the seeds for discontent quickly sprout. Close timing of the interdependence contributes to this frustration. If there is little temporal slack between the parties, the chances are greater that one or both of them will not complete their tasks in the allotted time; thus, the chances of frustrating the other's goal attainment increases.

The environment and the interdependent parties' specialization also contribute to interdependence difficulties. When the environment becomes uncertain, the probability of a unit's completing its facet of the task is lowered; thus, the unit increasingly frustrates its dependent counterpart. For example, Stilwell found his relationship with the Air

Corps extremely frustrating whenever changing weather conditions precluded supply deliveries over the hump and close air support for his beleaguered troops.

Specialization also contributes to interdependence difficulties. With a high degree of specialization, only the counterpart can complete the task upon which the party is dependent; with less specialization, the party might be able to complete not only its task, but also, if the need should arise, the tools of its counterpart.

Differences in Goals • The impact of differences in goals on conflict resolution is intuitively clear: they align parties against each other. For example, the PLO wants to destroy Israel, and Israel (not surprisingly) wants to survive; therefore, there is a high probability of conflict between them. Likewise, Somalia and Ethiopia probably will continue their conflict as long as they both have as their goal the possession of the same territory.

Several factors contribute to the goal differences. Perhaps most important is the reward system. Individuals, groups, and organizations are rewarded for the pursuit and attainment of their own goals. Thus, they continue to concentrate on and seek these goals. By chance, many of these goals conflict; thus, as parties strive for their goals, they find themselves in competition with others.

In many societies, and in ours particularly, competition within and between organizations is directly reinforced. In fact, past reinforcement has established a competition norm within our society. If you disagree, ask yourself this question: To what extent do I suffer from the Patton or Lombardi syndrome? That is, do you "love a winner"? Do you feel that "winning isn't everything; it's the only thing"? And do you agree with Don Meredith when he says, "Show me a good loser and I'll show you a loser"? Most of us enjoy competition. We have participated in competitive sports since we can remember, and in these we have been reinforced for victory. We all like to win; it is fun, and although it is not everything, losing is nothing.

In some cases, competition and even conflict are encouraged for more functional reasons. Organizations may encourage competition in order to stimulate their employees. Such competition is felt to eliminate boredom, bring out the novelty of divergent opinions (Thomas, 1976), stimulate interest, seed curiosity, and underpin the active use of people's capacities.

Competition also often produces ideas of high quality. Disagreements force people to be aware of different perspectives, different criteria, divergent values, and so on. Thus, competition forces parties to consider factors previously ignored, to be more creative, to exchange ideas with others, and to synthesize these ideas with their own. Via another route, competition also leads to these high-quality products. The active competitive pursuit at times leads to deadlocks and conflict; since these results are frustrating to the participating parties, they search for ways to circumvent the deadlocks and reduce the conflict. Such searches frequently improve the relationship between parties, benefit other parties with whom they are associated, and lay a constructive groundwork for future relations.

Conflict often is encouraged to test people and improve systems. People who promote competition with this goal in mind believe that such competition will lead to the survival of the fittest, the steeling of the wills of the survivors, and the polishing of the rough gems of loyalty. Although there is little evidence to support these notions, there are sufficient data showing that the fostering of competition and conflict with external entities does provide one positive benefit, the internal cohesiveness of the group (Blake & Mouton, 1961).

As do competitive rewards and differences in individual goals, dependences on limited resources also promote goal differences. Whenever resources are sufficient, the goal differences are less salient and evoke less conflict. As resource scarcity increases, the differences become more prominent and more likely to evoke difficulties.

Differences in Perceptions • The final direct source of conflict is the differences in the parties' perceptions of reality. To appreciate the role played by perceptions, keep in mind that perceptions are reality for each party. Thus, differences in perception understandably lead to disagreement; poor communication; insensitivity to the other's position; and, eventually, to competition and conflict.

To a large extent, different perceptions spring from specialization and the division of labor. A study by Dearborn and Simon (1958) provides a fine illustration of the effects of specialization. Middle executives with a variety of roles—marketing, accounting, production, and so on—were asked to read a rather lengthy business case. Having read the case, each was asked to note the major problem facing the firm. Their replies, not unsurprisingly, correlated highly with their roles (that is, marketing managers mentioned marketing problems; production, production problems; and so on). In general, the managers' perceptions were determined by their area of specialization.

The relationship between specialization and perceptual differences is supported by three links: differences in time horizons, differences in information sources, and differences in information channels.

Perceptions of the tasks we undertake are strongly affected by our time horizon. A person in the carpe diem age no doubt saw life very differently than does one of us, who in this age of planning and computers has been educated to consider the long-run effects of our actions. Probably both we and our carpe diem counterparts perceive tasks differently than did John Maynard Keynes, who, while advocating tackling economic problems in the moderate run, muttered, "In the long run we're dead."

Consider how people's time horizons and thereby their perceptions might vary within a skyjacking negotiation. The airline official whose 747, pilots, crew, and passengers are being held perceives the negotiation from a short—day-to-day or hour-to-hour—time perspective. This official therefore perceives success as the release of the plane, pilots, crew, and passengers. In contrast, the head of internal security for the country perceives the negotiations from a long—year-to-year or month-to-month—perspective. Consequently, this person perceives success as the punishment of the skyjackers. As a result of the differences between the airline official's and the security official's tasks, time horizons, and resultant perspectives, disagreement is expected between them as they provide inputs to the negotiation.

Specialization not only leads to different time perspectives; it also creates independent sources of information, with each specialist turning to parties that can provide information the specialty needs, can use, and can understand. Since different information is required and understood by each specialist, they each devise and/or become dependent upon highly specialized information schemes that differ from those with different fortes. Thus, their information tends to differ; their information sources differ; and, not surprisingly, their resultant perceptions vary.

Even though the information source may be the same, the information supplied to each party may differ. This is particularly true in organizations. To reduce overload on the various segments and personnel, organizational administrations filter information flowing to the units such that the relevant information is passed along only to the units that have "the need to know." Since this channeling results in different information going to different specialties, the specialized units in turn pick up different perceptions and assign different priorities to the tasks before them.

In summary, it has been argued that conflict is spawned by three main sources—party interdependence, differences in goals, and differences in perceptions—and, as we will see, the process engendered is a complex, cyclical one that can be managed effectively with negotiations.

Conflict Process

Probably one of the best overviews of the conflict process is presented by Thomas (1976). Drawing on the works of Pondy (1967) and Walton (1969), Thomas notes that the conflict cycle is composed of multiple episodes, each made up of five major events: frustration of goal attainment, conceptualization, behavior, the other's reactions, and outcome (Exhibit 7–3). Drawing upon our previous argument, we can consider the interdependence, differences in goals, and differences in perceptions as the precursors of the first episode. These factors foster the other's behavior and subsequent outcomes frustrating to the party's goal attainment. As the party conceptualizes the situation, the frustration or conflict becomes salient to her, and she then undertakes behavior to rectify the frustration. In turn, the other party reacts to the behavior, and this reaction serves as a stimulus for the party's next response. This cycle continues within the episode, with each party's behavior serving as a response to and a stimulus for the other's responses.

Other, perhaps more cognitive, elements are also indigenous to the unfolding stimulus-response cycle. As the frustration and resultant competitiveness mount, the party's judgments become biased and communication with the other party, lowered. The biased party starts to perceive herself and her group in highly favorable terms, whereas she perceives the other party unfavorably. The communications channel is not only infrequently used; the messages over it become more abusive than conciliatory. These biased perceptions and reduced, negative communications, occurring simultaneously, reinforce each other. Since the party has a high opinion of herself and a low opinion of the other, she does not wish to communicate with or waste amenities upon the other. And since her interactions with the other party remain low, the party has no basis for changing her perception of the other. As a result of this biased perception–reduced communication interaction, the two parties, in their conceptualizations, behaviors, and reactions, not only generate outcomes that are frustrating to each other; they also develop highly deleterious attitudes toward each other. They retaliate against each other's retaliation, polarizing farther and farther from each other in terms of perceptions, goals, and attitudes.

From the emotion-laden cycle of conceptualization, behavior,

Exhibit 7–3. Conflict Process.

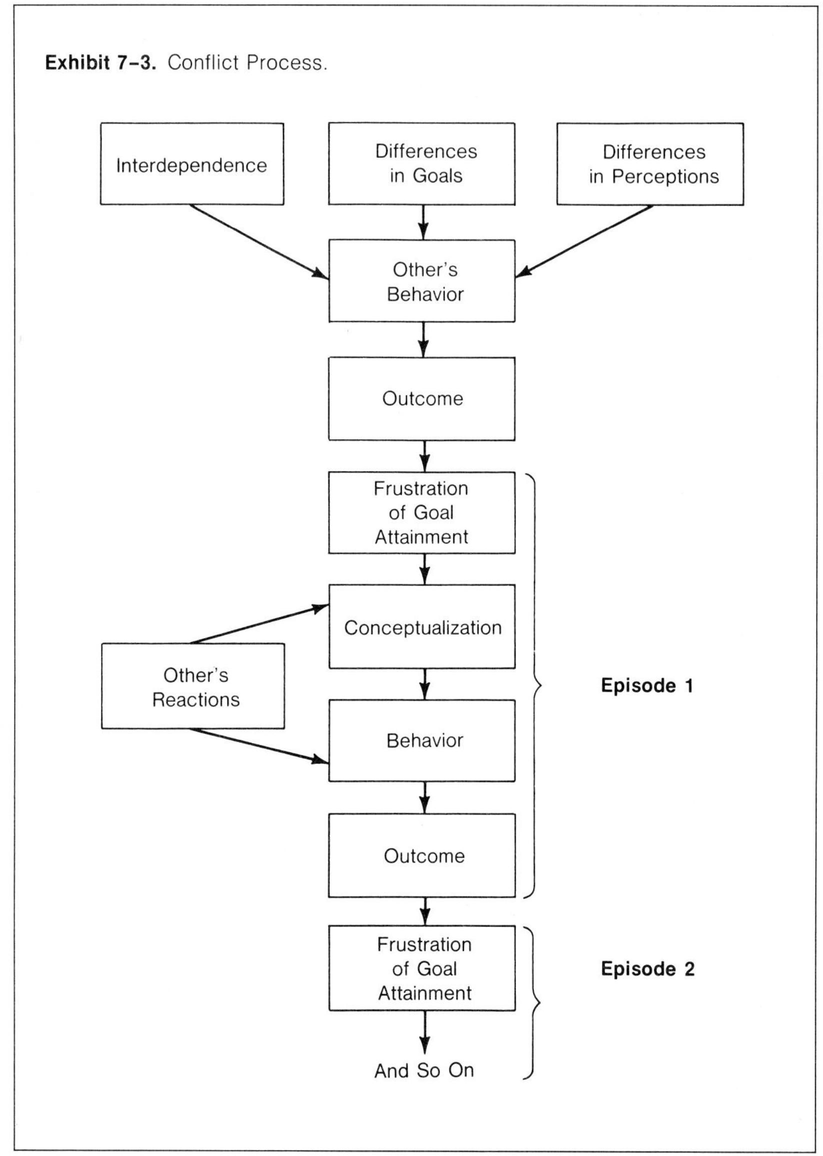

other's reactions, conceptualization, and so on flows harmful outcomes, as well as unrealized potential joint outcomes. In Episode 2 the cycle continues, Episode 3 follows, and so on until one party is victorious and the other is defeated or until a hostile stalemate prevails. Perhaps the parties will complete the conflict process with a joint agreement, a joint avoidance of the issues, or a withdrawal to their respective corners.

Negotiations and Conflict • Enter negotiations. Although conflict does have some beneficial effects, others that are pernicious call for its management. Negotiation, because of its impact on the causes, interactions, and outcomes of conflict, serves as a superb technique for managing conflict.

Recall that interdependence—one cause of conflict—results from mutual dependence on limited resources and interdependence in the timing of activities. Negotiation can reduce the impact of these two factors and thereby their indirect contribution to conflict.

Mutual dependence on limited resources can be addressed in several ways. The first is via a negotiation to determine how the mutual resources are to be jointly used. Each party can reveal her needs, come to understand those of the other, and better understand the extent to which her needs and those of the other are mutually exclusive. Having gleaned this information, the parties then can negotiate or jointly decide on a joint use of the resources. Perhaps they will agree upon concomitant use of the same resource. For example, a truck from a jointly used motor pool can pick up parts for both departments at a distant warehouse. Scheduling of separate uses also is possible. For example, surfers can use the water from six to ten o'clock in the morning and from four to eight o'clock in the evening, and swimmers have command at the other times. A combination of concomitant and separate uses also is possible. For instance, in Europe many saunas are used on this basis: Males use the facility at one time; females, at another; and at specified times the sexes sweat jointly. If the resources are divisible, the parties can alternatively reduce or eliminate their interdependence by negotiating a division of a resource, as do administrators who hammer out budgets for the departments in their organizations.

Since the interdependence in timing of activities is to a large extent created by the parties or their administrators, negotiations can modify the timing. For example, if Assembler B can complete his task only after Assembler A has completed hers, and they find that the timing is such that B constantly must wait for A to finish, A and B might negotiate an agreement whereby both A and B work on Task A until a sufficient inventory has been established. Then B will return to his task. In contrast, A and B might form a coalition and negotiate with their supervisor to obtain assistance for A in the completion of her task.

Negotiations also can affect differences in goals—the second cause of conflict. Direct, potent effects are possible, because negotiating parties tend to compromise their own goals and align their expectations with those of the other. Negotiation also eliminates the causes of different goals. As March and Simon (1958) note, reward systems in most organizations are the products of negotiations by the different units. Thus, to reduce or eliminate the competitiveness of the reward systems, the negotiating units need to hammer out systems that not only please the various units, but also foster cooperation among them.

Negotiation probably has its most significant impact by aligning the parties' perceptions. In a negotiation, a great deal of information is exchanged; the parties provide information favoring their views and goals, as well as the criteria for the alternatives they have chosen and rejected. Simultaneously, each party also provides information about the other's views, goals, criteria, and alternatives in attempts to contradict the other's arguments and block his goal attainment. In this informational give-and-take or defense-and-attack, each party learns a great deal not only about the other's goals, attitudes, perceptions, and preferences, but also about his own. And as the parties do so, they begin to perceive their own ideas, goals, preferences, and attitudes from the other's point of view and also to perceive the other's from his point of view. The improved perceptions and enhanced comprehension do not necessarily align the parties' goals, but they do clear away many of the misunderstandings and other irrational factors that can spawn difficulties.

Negotiation controls some of the conflict causes and enhances communication within the process; it also precludes or substitutes for the party's aggressive behavior and the other's parallel reactions. Likewise, negotiation allows parties to reduce their anxieties by talking, threatening, insulting, and being listened to. At times, even when it does not eliminate the frustration of goal attainment, it does reduce it. It also highlights the costs of the full cycle of conflict that the party will face if she ventures into the conflict arena.

Once conflict has cycled through a few episodes, negotiation can prove invaluable by substituting for advanced conflict, placing limits on it, or facilitating its reduction. Herein lies the joker in the negotiation deck: negotiation can be used late in the conflict to cut losses, even though it was not used earlier. Perhaps herein also lies its handicap: negotiation is always a backup used before, during, or after conflict rather than a brief opportunity that must be seized immediately or lost forever. Because of its continuous availability, negotiation often falls victim to procrastination, leaving the combatants and their victims poorer, but seldom wiser.

Nuclear Conflict

Prior to ending a chapter entitled "Negotiations Applied" or closing a discussion on conflict resolution negotiations, our attention must turn to the most important conflict: nuclear. The immediately preceding pages discussed ways in which negotiations can control conflict; end it; reduce its costs; and, after a cycle or so, substitute for it. In a nuclear conflict—the most costly of all conflicts—negotiation ironically can perform none of these vital functions; there simply is neither time nor opportunity for negotiation. As Jonathan Schell (1982) concludes in his forceful book, *The Fate of the Earth*, once a nuclear war breaks out, there will be no way to limit it. The escalation and the speed with which it takes place will doom not only the chances of fruitful negotiation, but also the earth, the ecosystem, military game plans, and political processes. Perhaps this is not true; perhaps the opposing sides can undertake a negotiation in the midst of a holocaust. However, that seems unlikely. The many "irresolvable uncertainties" of the nuclear conflict assure us that it might happen, and, since it might, we have no right to gamble. If we lose, we lose it all—ourselves, our earth, and our future generations—and we do not get to play a second round.

Given that a nuclear conflict is less than desirable and that there is an unacceptably high risk that nothing—including negotiations—can constrain, limit, or terminate it, it seems prudent and obvious that we should undertake measures such as negotiations to lower the probability of its occurrence. Currently, the nuclear powers are negotiating to preclude a nuclear conflict, yet they are doing so ineffectively; the reasons for this difficulty appear to be threefold. First, the need for negotiation is not being taken seriously. Both major nuclear powers are giving higher priority to gaining technological advantages over the opponent than to negotiating effectively with the opponent. As they do so, they operate under the absurd assumption that by preparing for war, they can end it. An even stronger detriment to the effectiveness of negotiation appears to be the public's numbness. Most U.S. and Soviet citizens do not think about the potential holocaust; they distance themselves from the reality that currently there are 50,000 warheads in the world that possess destruction capabilities 1.6 million times that of the bomb dropped on Hiroshima.

A third, complementary contributor to the observed negotiation ineffectiveness is the nuclear powers' poor negotiating. Frequently we observe signs of this: diplomats employing the same tactics regardless of the circumstances; Vance's revelation to Dobrynin of his backup offer; Gromyko's overaggressiveness when the United States held a weak bargaining deck. What are the roots of the poor negotiations? One appears to be the United States' change in negotiators with every administration. Such alterations bring changes in goals, tactics, personalities, and strategies that no doubt confuse opponents and place them on the defensive. Across the table, the Soviets have relied redundantly on the same negotiators and strategies, debasing both with overuse.

A second cause of poor negotiations is that the negotiators do not know how to negotiate. This is not to say that the U.S. and Soviet negotiators are not aware of and exploiting the current state of the art. These negotiations probably are some of the best in the world. Rather, this condemnation targets the state of the art. The science of negotiation is not proffering its potential; therefore, the negotiators are not negotiating as well as they could. Progress in negotiation, as in the social sciences, has not only been outstripped by that in the natural sciences; it also has been retarded by natural science advances. Advances in the natural sciences have fostered funds flows into those areas, diverting some from the social sciences. In addition, society, with the breakthrough in nuclear weapons, has tended to become inept. It is not that society has difficulty using the current social mechanisms—among them negotiations—to deal with the new scientific development; it is that the potential horror of the weapons numbs us or sets us back in our capability to deal with opponents.

As a result of assigning low priority to negotiations and failure to devote ample resources toward the study and improvement of negotiations, society has inadvertently developed a bias against negotiation. Negotiation does not work; therefore, society prefers to put its faith in science and its resources into more accurate delivery systems, better detection devices, and larger warhead yields.

Such an attitude was reflected in a friend's question to me the other day: "How can you negotiate with people you don't trust?" I responded: "When they are as strong as you, that is the only way you can deal with them."

To increase the effectiveness of negotiation in avoiding conflict and serving its other multifaceted functions, we need to alter this attitude, to improve the art and science of negotiation, and thereby to improve the practice of negotiation. It is hoped that this book contributes toward these goals.

Epilogue

● A fundamental of journalism is that the reporter must tell the people what they are to hear, let them hear it, and then tell them what they have heard. To this point the first two facets have been provided; as a conclusion, the third is provided here—the overriding thesis has been that negotiation is useful. This was argued generally and specifically in Chapter 1, in some detail in Chapter 7, and tacitly by use of examples in the remaining chapters.

Chapter 1 began with a delineation of the negotiation process, which was followed by an overview of the negotiation stages and an enumeration of the determinants of the negotiator's behavior. Chapter 2 mapped out a general understanding of three processes—maneuvers, tactics, and strategies—and Chapters 3 through 5 analyzed each in detail. Chapter 6 argued that a negotiator, in choosing a strategy, must match it correctly with the situation. The various aspects of the negotiation situation were explored, and then attention was focused on the situational impact on strategy development. Finally, Chapter 7 presented the capstone: arguments that negotiation is useful in interpersonal relations, intergroup relations, decision making, group leadership, MBO, turnover control, vertical and horizontal organizational integration, interorganizational relationships, and conflict resolution.

References

Adams, J. S. (1965). Inequity in social exchange. In L. Berkowitz (Ed)., *Advances in experimental social psychology* (pp. 267–299). New York: Academic Press.

Alpern, D. M. (1980, July 28). How the Ford deal collapsed. *Newsweek*, pp. 20–26. An answer for Tehran. (1980, November). *Time*, p. 42.

Bartos, O. J. (1967). How predictable are negotiations? *Journal of Conflict Resolution, 11*, 481–496.

Bartos, O. J. (1970). Determinants and consequences of toughness. In P. Swingle (Ed.), *The structure of conflict* (pp. 45–68). New York: Academic Press.

Bass, B. M. (1966). Effects on the subsequent performance of negotiators of studying issues or planning strategies alone or in groups. *Psychological Monographs, 80* (Whole No. 614).

Blake, R. R., & Mouton, J. S. (1961). Comprehension of own and of outgroup positions under intergroup competition. *Journal of Conflict Resolution, 5*, 304–310.

Brecher, J. (1980, November 24). East is east and west is west. *Newsweek*, pp. 77–78.

Brown, B. R. (1977). Face-saving and face restoration in negotiation. In D. Druckman (Ed.), *Negotiations* (pp. 275–299). Beverly Hills, CA: Sage.

Cancio, H. A. (1959). Some reflections on the role of mediation. *Labor Law Journal, 10,* 720–723.

Chertkoff, J. M., & Conley, M. (1967). Opening offer and frequency of concession as bargaining strategies. *Journal of Personality and Social Psychology, 7*, 181–185.

Chipman, J. S. (1965). A survey of the theory of international trade: 2. The neoclassical theory. *Econometrica, 33*, 685–760.

Church, G. J. (1981, February 2). An end to the long ordeal. *Time*, pp. 24–34.

Conrath, D. W. (1970). Experience as a factor in experimental gaming behavior. *Journal of Conflict Resolution, 14*, 195–202.

Crow, W. J., & Noel, W. (1965). *The valid use of simulation results* (Contract No. CA-49-146-XZ-110). Report presented to the Western Behavioral Sciences Institute, La Jolla, CA.

Dansereau, F., Graen, G., & Haga, W. J. (1975). A vertical linkage approach to leadership within formal organizations: A longitudinal investigation of the role making process. *Organizational Behavior and Human Performance, 13*, 46–78.

Dearborn, D. C., & Simon, H. A. (1958). Selective perception: A note on the departmental identification of executives. *Sociometry, 21*, 140–144.

Deutsch, M. (1973). *The resolution of conflict: Constructive and destructive processes*. New Haven, CT: Yale University Press.

Douglas, A. (1957). The peaceful settlement of industrial and inter-group disputes. *Journal of Conflict Resolution, 1*, 69–81.

Douglas, A. (1962). *Industrial peacemaking*. New York: Columbia University Press.

Drucker, P. F. (1954). *The practice of management*. New York: Harper & Row.

Druckman, D., Zechmeister, K., & Soloman, D. (1972). Determinants of bargaining behavior in a bilateral monopoly situation: Opponent's concession rate and relative defensibility. *Behavioral Science, 17*, 514–531.

Dunlop, J. T., & Healy, J. J. (1955). *Collective bargaining: Principles and cases.* Homewood, IL: Irwin.

Ellsberg, D. (1975). The theory and practice of blackmail. In O. R. Young (Ed.), *Bargaining* (pp. 343–363). Urbana: University of Illinois Press.

Esser, J. K., & Komorita, S. S. (1975). Reciprocity and concession making in bargaining. *Journal of Personality and Social Psychology, 31*, 864–872.

Fisher, R., & Ury, W. (1981). *Getting to yes*. Boston: Houghton Mifflin.

Galbraith, J. (1977). *Organizational design*. Reading, MA: Addison-Wesley.

Gest, T. (1981, August 24). Soaring costs of civil suits: The lawyers' answer. *U.S. News and World Report*, p. 52.

Gouldner, A. W. (1960). The norm of reciprocity: A preliminary statement. *American Sociological Review, 25*, 161–178.

Graen, G., Dansereau, F., Haga, W., & Cashman, J. (1975). *The invisible organization*. Boston: Schenkman.

Haga, W. J., Graen, G., & Dansereau, F. (1974). Professionalism and role making in a service organization: A longitudinal investigation. *American Sociological Review, 39*, 122–133.

Hamner, W. D. (1974). Effects of bargaining strategy and pressure to reach agreement in a stalemated negotiation. *Journal of Personality and Social Psychology, 30*, 458–467.

Harnett, D. L., & Cummings, L. L. (1980). *Bargaining behavior*. Houston: Dame Publishing.

Harrison, A. A., & McClintock, C. G. (1965). Previous experience within the dyad and cooperative game behavior. *Journal of Personality and Social Psychology, 1*, 671–675.

Harsanyi, J. C. (1962). Bargaining in ignorance of the opponent's utility function. *Journal of Conflict Resolution, 6*, 29–38.

Hell no, I won't go! (1980, July 21). *Time*, p. 55.

Homans, G. C. (1961). *Social behavior: Its elementary forms*. New York: Harcourt Brace Jovanovich.

Hornstein, H. A., & Deutsch, M. (1967). Tendencies to compete and to attack as a function of inspection, incentive, and available alternatives. *Journal of Personality and Social Psychology, 5*, 311–318.

Iklé, F. C. (1964). *How nations negotiate*. New York: Harper & Row.

Johnson, D. W. (1967). The use of role-reversal in intergroup competition. *Journal of Personality and Social Psychology, 7*, 135–142.

Joseph, M. L., & Wilks, R. H. (1963). An experimental analog to two-party bargaining. *Behavioral Science, 8*, 117–127.

Kelley, H. H., & Schenitzki, D. B. (1972). Bargaining. In C. G. McClintock (Ed.), *Experimental social psychology* (pp. 298–337). New York: Holt.

Kissinger, H. (1979). *White House Years*. Boston: Little, Brown.

Klimoski, R. J. (1972). The effects of intragroup forces on intergroup conflict resolution. *Organizational Behavior and Human Performance, 8*, 363–383.

Klimoski, R. J., & Ash, R. A. (1974). Accountability and negotiator behavior. *Organizational Behavior and Human Performance, 11*, 409–425.

Kochan, T. A. (1980). *Collective bargaining and industrial relations*. Homewood, IL: Irwin.

Komorita, S. S., & Barnes, M. Effects of pressures to reach agreement in bargaining. (1969). *Journal of Personality and Social Psychology, 13*, 245–252.

Komorita, S. S., & Brenner, A. R. (1968). Bargaining and concession making under bilateral monopoly. *Journal of Personality and Social Psychology, 9*, 15–20.

Kruglanski, A. W. (1970). Attributing trustworthiness in supervisor-worker relations. *Journal of Experimental Social Psychology, 6*, 214–232.

Lall, A. (1966). *Modern international negotiation: Principles and practice*. New York: Columbia University Press.

Liebert, R. M., Smith, W. P., Hill, J. H., & Keiffer, M. (1968). The effects of information and magnitude of initial offer on interpersonal negotiation. *Journal of Experimental Social Psychology, 4*, 431–441.

Likert, R. (1961). *New patterns of management*. New York: McGraw-Hill.

Lindskold, S., Bennett, R., & Wagner, M. (1976). *Influencing cooperation with explicit communication of norms, objectives, and strategic intentions*. Unpublished manuscript, Ohio University, Athens.

Magnusan, E. (1981, January 26). Hostage breakthrough. *Time*, pp. 13–19.

Maier, N. R. F. (1973). *Psychology in industrial organizations* (4th ed.). Boston: Houghton Mifflin.

March, J. G., & Simon, H. A. (1958). *Organizations*. New York: Wiley.

McClintock, C. G., & McNeel, S. P. (1967). Prior dyadic experience and monetary reward as determinants of cooperative and competitive game behavior. *Journal of Personality and Social Psychology, 5*, 282–294.

Midgaard, K., & Underdal, A. (1977). Multiparty conferences. In D. Druckman (Ed.), *Negotiations* (pp. 329–345). Beverly Hills, CA: Sage.

Mintzberg, H. (1973). *The nature of managerial work*. New York: Harper & Row.

Mobley, W. H., Griffeth, R. W., Hand, H. H., & Meglino, B. M. (1979). Review and conceptual analysis of the employee turnover process. *Psychological Bulletin, 86*, 493–522.

Morley, I., & Stephenson, G. (1977). *The social psychology of bargaining*. London: George Allen and Univan.

An offer Iran can refuse. (1980, November 24). *Newsweek*, p. 72.

Osgood, C. E. (1959). Suggestions for winning the real war with Communism. *Journal of Conflict Resolution, 3*, 295–325.

Osgood, C. E. (1962). *An alternative to war or surrender*. Urbana: University of Illinois Press.

Peters, E. (1955). *Strategy and tactics in labor negotiations*. New London, CT: National Foremen's Institute.

Philip Morris and Rothman's join forces. (1981, April 23). *Winston-Salem Journal*, p. 2.

Polish union votes to ready for strike. (1981, March 24). *Columbia* (Missouri) *Tribune*, p. 1.

Pondy, L. R. (1967). Organizational conflict: Concepts and models. *Administrative Science Quarterly, 12*, 296–320.

Porter, L. W., Crampon, W. J., & Smith, F. J. (1976). Organizational commitment and managerial turnover: A longitudinal study. *Organizational Behavior and Human Performance, 15*, 87–98.

Pruitt, D. G. (1968). Reciprocity and credit building in a laboratory dyad. *Journal of Personality and Social Psychology, 8*, 143–147.

Pruitt, D. G. (1971). Indirect communication and the search for agreement in negotiation. *Journal of Applied Social Psychology, 1*, 205–238.

Pruitt, D. G., & Drews, J. L. (1969). The effect of time pressure, time elapsed, and the opponent's concession rate on behavior in negotiation. *Journal of Experimental Social Psychology, 5*, 43–60.

Pruitt, D. G., & Johnson, D. F. (1970). Mediation as an aid to face saving in negotiation. *Journal of Personality and Social Psychology, 14*, 239–246.

Pruitt, D. G., & Kimmel, M. J. (1977). Twenty years of experimental gaming: Critique, synthesis, and suggestions for the future. *Annual Review of Psychology, 28*, 363–392.

Pruitt, D. G., & Lewis, S. A. (1977). The psychology of integrative bargaining. In D. Druckman (Ed.), *Negotiations* (pp. 161–192). Beverly Hills, CA: Sage.

Quinn, R., Seashore, S., Kahn, R., Mangione, T., Campbell, D. Staines, G., & McCullough, M. (1971). *Survey of working conditions, 1969–1970* (Document No. 2916-0001). Washington, D.C.: U.S. Government Printing Office.

Raio, A. P. (1974). *Managing by objectives*. Glenview, IL: Scott, Foresman.

Rubin, J. Z., & Brown, B. R. (1975). *The social psychology of bargaining and negotiation*. New York: Academic Press.

Rubin, J. Z., & Dimatteo, M. R. (1972). Factors affecting the magnitude of subjective ability parameters in a tacit bargaining game. *Journal of Experimental Social Psychology, 8*, 412–426.

Sagan, C. (1980). *Cosmos*. New York: Random House.

Sanders, Lawrence. (1978). *The tangent factor*. New York: Putnam.

Sawyer, J., & Guetzkow, H. (1965). Bargaining and negotiation in international relations. In H. C. Kelman (Ed.), *International behavior and social psychological analysis* (pp. 466–520). New York: Holt.

Sayles, L. R. (1964). *Managerial behavior: Administration in complex organizations*. New York: McGraw-Hill.

Schell, J. (1982). *The fate of the earth*. New York: Knopf.

Schelling, T. C. (1960). *The strategy of conflict*. New York: Harvard University Press.

Schorff, E. E. (1981, February 2). How the bargain was struck. *Time*, pp. 37–38.

Siegel, S., & Fouraker, L. E. (1960). *Bargaining and group decision making: Experiments in bilateral monopoly*. New York: McGraw-Hill.

Sigal, L. V. (1979). *Reporters and officials*. Lexington, MA: Heath.

Skinner, B. F. (1969). *Contingencies of reinforcement: A theoretical analysis*. Englewood Cliffs, NJ: Prentice-Hall.

Skow, J. (1981, January 26). The long ordeal of the hostages. *Time*, pp. 20–24.

Smith, S. (1980, November 24). Another victory for solidarity. *Time*, pp. 49–50.

South Africa's mystery man: Anton E. Rupert. (1974, September 28). *Business Week*, pp. 80–85.

Soviet government newspaper hails SALT agreement. (1979, May 13). *Washington Post*.

Steele, R. (1977, April 11). Testing Carter. *Newsweek*, pp. 26–30.

Steers, R. M. (1977). Antecedents and outcomes of organizational commitment. *Administrative Science Quarterly, 22*, 46–56.

Stevens, C. M. (1963). *Strategy and collective bargaining negotiation*. New York: McGraw-Hill.

Strauss, A. (1978). *Negotiations*. San Francisco: Jossey-Bass.

Strickland, L. H. (1958). Surveillance and trust. *Journal of Personality, 26*, 200–215.

Tactical concepts of Lin Piao. (1951, December 31). *Life*, pp. 21–22.

Talbott, S. (1980a, November 10). Hope for the hostages. *Time*, pp. 14–16.

Talbott, S. (1980b, November 17). Hoping for a homecoming. *Time*, pp. 74–76.

Talks may bring merger of RJR, African company. (1981, April 3). *Winston-Salem Journal*, p. 1.

Taylor, A. (1981, February 2). How the bankers did it. *Time*, pp. 56–58.

Tedeschi, J. T., & Bonoma, T. V. (1977). Measures of last resort: Coercion and aggression in bargaining. In D. Druckman (Ed.), *Negotiations* (pp. 213–241). Beverly Hills, CA: Sage.

Tedeschi, J. T., Bonoma, T. V., & Novinson, H. (1970). Behavior of a threatener: Retaliation vs. fixed opportunity costs. *Journal of Conflict Resolution, 14*, pp. 69–76.

Thibaut, J. W., & Kelley, H. H. (1959). *The social psychology of groups*. New York: Wiley.

Thomas, K. (1976). Conflict and conflict management. In M. D. Dunnette (Ed.), *Handbook of industrial and organizational psychology* (pp. 889–935). Chicago: Rand McNally.

Thompson, J. D. (1967). *Organizations in action*. New York: McGraw-Hill.

Vroom, V. H., & Yetton, P. W. (1973). *Leadership and decision-making*. Pittsburgh: University of Pittsburgh Press.

Walcott, C., Hopman, P. T., & King, T. D. (1977). The role of debate in negotiation. In D. Druckman (Ed.), *Negotiations* (pp. 193–212). Beverly Hills, CA: Sage.

Wall, J. A. (1977). Operantly conditioning a negotiator's concession-making. *Journal of Experimental Social Psychology, 13*, 431–440.

Wall, J. A. (1981a). An investigation of reciprocity and reinforcement theories of bargaining behavior. *Organizational Behavior and Human Performance, 27*, 367–385.

Wall, J. A. (1981b). Mediation: An analysis, review, and proposed research. *Journal of Conflict Resolution, 25*, 157–180.

Walton, R. E. (1969). *Interpersonal peacemaking: Confrontations and third party consultation*. Reading, MA: Addison-Wesley.

Walton, R. E., & McKersie, R. B. (1965). *A behavioral theory of labor negotiations: An analysis of a social interaction system*. New York: McGraw-Hill.

Warren, R., Rose, S., & Bergunder, A. (1974). *The structure of urban reform*. Lexington, MA: Heath.

Westmoreland, J. (1981, April 23). Philip Morris deal leaves RJR stunned. *Twin City Sentinel* (Winston-Salem, NC), p. 12.

Who conceded what to whom. (1979, May 21). *Time*, pp. 25–35.

Yukl, G. A. (1972a). The effect of opponent concessions on a bargainer's perception and concessions. *Proceedings of the 80th Annual Convention of the American Psychological Association*, pp. 229–230.

Yukl, G. A. (1972b). *Effects of opponent's initial offer and concession trend under partial information*. Unpublished manuscript, University of Akron, Akron, Ohio.

Yukl, G. A. (1973). The effects of the opponent's initial offer and concession magnitude on bargaining outcomes. *Proceedings of the 81st Annual Convention of the American Psychological Association*, pp. 143–144.

Yukl, G. A. (1974a). Effects of the opponent's initial offer, concession magnitude, and concession frequency on bargaining behavior. *Journal of Personality and Social Psychology, 30*, 332–335.

Yukl, G. A. (1974b). The effects of situational variables and opponent concessions on a bargainer's perception, aspirations, and concessions. *Journal of Personality and Social Psychology, 29*, 227–236.

Yukl, G. A. (1976). *A review of laboratory research on two-party negotiations*. Unpublished manuscript, Baruch College, Wayne State University, Detroit.

Index